# Classroom Management Simplified

### Elizabeth Breaux

EYE ON EDUCATION
6 DEPOT WAY WEST, SUITE 106
LARCHMONT, NY 10538
(914) 833–0551
(914) 833–0761 fax
www.eyeoneducation.com

Library of Congress Cataloging-in-Publication Data

Breaux, Elizabeth, 1961-
   Classroom management simplified / Elizabeth Breaux.
      p. cm.
   ISBN 1-59667-001-0
   1.  Classroom management.  I. Title.
   LB3013.B675 2005
   371.102'4—dc22

                                                     2004030792

10 9 8 7 6 5 4 3

Editorial and production services provided by
Richard H. Adin Freelance Editorial Services
52 Oakwood Blvd., Poughkeepsie, NY 12603-4112
(845-471-3566)

## *Also Available from* EYE ON EDUCATION

**REAL Teachers, REAL Challenges, REAL Solutions:**
**25 Ways to Handle the Challenges of the Classroom Effectively**
Annette L. Breaux and Elizabeth Breaux

**101 "Answers" for New Teachers and Their Mentors:**
**Effective Teaching Tips for Daily Classroom Use**
Annette L. Breaux

**The Poetry of Annette Breaux**
Annette Breaux

**What Great Teachers Do *Differently***
**14 Things That Matter Most**
Todd Whitaker

**Teaching Matters: Motivating & Inspiring Yourself**
Todd and Beth Whitaker

**Dealing with Difficult Parents**
**(And with Parents in Difficult Situations)**
Todd Whitaker and Douglas J. Fiore

**Great Quotes for Great Educators**
Todd Whitaker and Dale Lumpa

**Handbook on Differentiated Instruction**
**For Middle and High Schools**
Sheryn Spencer Northey

**Differentiated Instruction:**
**A Guide for Middle and High School Teachers**
Amy Benjamin

**Differentiated Instruction:**
**A Guide for Elementary School Teachers**
Amy Benjamin

**What Every Teacher Needs to Know About Assessment,**
**Second Edition**
Leslie Wilson

## *Dedication*

I dedicate this book to the two Annettes…

First, to Annette Breaux: my sister, my friend, my mentor, and the greatest teacher I have ever known. Thank you for your enthusiasm, your humor, your ongoing support, your undying love, and your unselfish devotion.

And to the "original" Annette Breaux—Mom: my grandmother, my most avid supporter and greatest fan. You taught me through example that possessing the ability to be optimistic amidst all obstacles was my key to the world. Thank you for charting the way and paving the road, so that now in your absence, I see all paths clearly. I miss you—no words can suffice…

# About the Author

Elizabeth Breaux is one of the most practical, down-to-earth, informative, and entertaining speakers and authors in the field of education. She leaves the members of her audiences laughing, crying, and certain that they have chosen the right profession—teaching.

She has taught and worked with at-risk students for 20 years and believes that there is not a more challenging and rewarding job in the world. Her message has always been a simple one: "I cannot teach my students until I reach my students."

A curriculum coordinator and former classroom teacher, she is also one of the coordinators of T.I.P.S., an induction program for new teachers in Lafayette, Louisiana. In addition, she trains new-teacher assessors for the Louisiana Department of Education.

Contact Education Speakers Group at www.educationspeakersgroup. com for information about hiring Ms. Breaux to speak to your school, district, or group.

# Foreword

### Six Teachers This Year

*Six teachers this year, what will I do?*
*What's good for one is not for two*
*Three says, "Go," but four says, "Stay"*
*And five's all work, while six is play*
*Now back to one and then to two*
*How will I know what I'm to do?*

*Elizabeth Breaux*

This book was written to provide to new teachers the benefits of veteran teachers' experiences, and to give veteran teachers that rejuvenating "shot in the arm" that we so often need. As veterans, many of us learned the hard way, by reinventing the wheel on a daily basis. Our first years of teaching were "sink or swim" situations. For those of us who lived to tell about it, we did swim. It wasn't a pretty sight. We bobbled, splashed, and choked, but we made it to the side! Because we were gluttons for punishment, we went back for more! (Many of our peers chose another path, never to be seen again in the teaching profession.)

We eventually learned that *consistency* was the key, and that our *approach* to all situations was what often determined the outcome. **Consistency** and **approach** are my two favorite words. I firmly believe that if you, the teacher, establish your rules and procedures from day one, and are consistent in their implementation, you will pave that smooth road for yourself much sooner than many of us ever did. I also know, through experience, that the manner in which any teacher approaches any situation is often the determining factor in the outcome of that situation. As teachers we have the ability and the power to lay the foundation on which success can be built in our classrooms. This book is filled with many "at your fingertips" solutions for doing just that.

It is my sincere desire to assist you in being the best teacher that you can possibly be, and to help you to arrive at the pinnacle of your profession in a timely fashion. Regardless of whom you teach, what you teach, or where you teach, the basic principles of this book apply to you. Stop reinventing the wheel. You truly can succeed from day one. Read on…

# Table of Contents

# Introduction

## Follow the Rules

*On the wall in big, bold words, were listed all the rules*

*The teacher warned that those who did not follow would be fools*

*One read, "Raise your hand to speak," another read, "Stay seated"*

*The third one read, "Don't ask to leave until your work's completed!"*

*The fourth and fifth and sixth and more I really don't recall*

*You see, the teacher failed to show what happened when we all*

*At any time would fail to follow any of the "rules"*

*It seems without consistency that she became the fool.*

*Elizabeth Breaux*

## What I've Learned About Classroom Management

- ◆ I've learned that a calm, caring, well-managed environment is the key to effective instruction.
- ◆ I've learned that effective management eliminates stress.
- ◆ I've learned that students *love* a well-managed, work-oriented, pleasant environment.
- ◆ I've learned that classroom management allows for the maximization of instructional time.
- ◆ I've learned that every student—every single one—is a worthwhile, teachable, and reachable individual who deserves a quality education.

## How to Use This Book

As the title implies, this book is structured in a very simple, easy-to-follow, user-friendly format that will allow immediate implementation and positive results. It's all spelled out for you.

It begins with Part I, "Procedures for Teachers," where you will find ten procedures that, if properly implemented, will make life in your classroom virtually stress-free. Each procedure includes an introduction and several tips for implementing the procedure, followed by a typical classroom scenario with both an effective and an ineffective way of handling it.

In Part II, "Procedures for Teachers and Their Students," you will find twenty-five procedures that you can begin implementing immediately in your classroom. Each procedure begins with a segment titled "How to Teach It" in which you will find specific instructions, including actual dialogue to use with your students in the teaching of the procedure. Following that is a segment titled "How to Practice It" that includes some fun activities to use in this practice phase. The final segment, "How to Implement It," explains how to implement the procedure immediately. No kidding: the very next day.

## What This Book Will Do for You

- If you are determined to maximize instructional time in your classroom
- If you are a dedicated teacher who believes that all students deserve a positive, structured, and chaos-free learning environment
- If you have struggled at times, as all teachers do, with implementing procedures and remaining consistent in that implementation
- If you are a new teacher or a veteran teacher looking for fresh ideas
- If you truly believe in treating all students with dignity, kindness, love, and consistency
- If you are an administrator looking to implement schoolwide procedures in a uniform, consistent manner on your campus
- If you are committed to reaching and teaching *all students*

## *This book will show you how!*

# Classroom Management Simplified

# Part I

# Procedures
# for Teachers

In Part I we discuss important procedures for teachers. In addition to an explanation of each procedure there is a section titled "Tips" that explains how to implement that procedure. Also included with each procedure is a typical classroom scenario followed by examples of effective implementation and ineffective implementation.

Read each scenario carefully and remember to laugh as you recognize yourself and some of your peers in these hypothetical cases. Remember that it is only when we can laugh at our own mistakes that we truly grow as professionals. If you are a veteran teacher, you've accrued years of laughable (and in some cases embarrassing) memories, some of which you wish you could erase. But don't forget that they were all valuable tools in the learning process. If you are a new teacher, be aware that you will be creating some laughable moments that will be remembered for years to come! Don't be so hard on yourself, however. We veterans only pretend that we have never made mistakes.

# Procedure 1 for Teachers:
# Organize Any Disorganization

### If I Survive

*I'm certain that I placed it there*
*I'm looking for it everywhere*
*Behind the doors and under chairs*
*Beneath the floor and in the air.*
*One day I will get organized*
*Next year sounds good (if I survive)*
*A better plan I must contrive*
*I'll do it tomorrow, if I'm alive!*

*Elizabeth Breaux*

"A place for everything, and everything in its place." Who said that? Was it my mother, my grandmother, Galileo, Copernicus? Does it really matter? It's so ingenious yet so basic. Live by it in the classroom, and life will be much less stressful.

An organized environment is a breeding ground for learning. We teachers therefore must become masters of organization if we are to become the masters of our classrooms. Learning cannot take place in a chaotic atmosphere. The bottom line is that if we are disorganized, we cannot command organization from our students. If the teacher is disorganized, the students will follow suit. Ultimately, learning will suffer dramatically. The good news is that the reverse is also true. Students really do love an organized learning environment, but it's up to the teacher to get the organizational ball rolling.

Organization begins long before the students arrive and continues long after they have "left the building." Don't leave the building until you organize your classroom!

## Tips for Becoming Organized

◆ Determine the amount of physical space you have and how to best organize that space for maximum efficiency.

- Arrange your own personal space first. Remember, *you live there.*
- Create rooms and/or stations within your classroom.
- Color-code everything.
- Create bins for everything. Bins should be clearly labeled.
- Create and display charts for everything: conduct chart, extra points chart, tardy chart, and so on. Make certain to assign numbers to students. Names should never be written on the charts.
- Label and/or color-code shelves, cubbyholes, and so on, by class (if you teach more than one class) and then by the materials that are stored there. Students then know what is off limits to them and what is not. They also know where items "live" in the classroom.
- Create supply boxes for your students. (More on this in Procedure 6 in Part II.) This works for all grade levels. Fill a small plastic box with necessary classroom supplies (pen, pencil, scissors, glue, ruler, eraser, crayons, compass, protractor, highlighter, calculator, etc.). Place one box in each desk. Write the name of every student who sits at that desk (if you teach more than one class) on the box. When students arrive, familiarize them with the supply boxes. Tell them that they are responsible for checking the box daily and telling the teacher immediately if anything is missing. This, of course, means that the student in the last class "accidentally" left with something that belongs in the box. The teacher then can retrieve the missing item. (The teacher will receive a reimbursement of sorts for the cost of the supplies because the students' supply lists include all or most of the items that are in the boxes. As students bring in their supplies, the teacher can collect and stockpile those items as replacements for the remainder of the year. There is usually a certain amount left over at the end of the year that is sufficient for creating the boxes for the next year.)
- Assign one student per row or group as the materials supervisor and show these students where *everything* lives. (See Procedure 7 in Part II.)
- Determine a space and/or place for everything. Don't deviate from this procedure. If an item is taken from its place, it must be returned to its place. No questions asked!

## Classroom Scenario

At this middle school the school day consists of six one-hour class periods. Students switch classes each hour. Teachers are given one planning period, but the remaining five class periods can be quite hectic, with one class rushing out as another rushes in.

### Teacher A

Teacher A signals to her class at 8:58 that the bell will ring in two minutes. She instructs the students to place all materials in the supply boxes. She motions to the materials supervisors to collect the materials and put them in their proper places. She reminds all the students to clear and collect all trash from their spaces. The teacher walks to the door and opens it. The bell rings, and the teacher quickly dismisses each row, beginning with the ones in which all the students have reorganized their spaces and returned all materials to their proper places. The students exit in an orderly fashion. An onlooker would notice that the room is impeccably neat, organized, and ready for the next class to enter (because rows are not dismissed until everything is in place). Miraculously, the teacher had nothing to do with returning the room to its original order (other than training the students to do it for her).

### Teacher B

The bells rings, and Teacher B is caught "off guard." Students are still in groups, and materials are scattered about. There is no obvious procedure for returning materials. Students begin frantically gathering their personal belongings and rushing out of the room. The teacher orders the students not to leave until all the materials have been returned, but few obey the teacher's "command." Desks are out of order, and supplies are everywhere. The students are racing to their next classes, and the teacher is frazzled. Unfortunately, another class is arriving, only to be greeted by this mass display of chaos.

---

**The fact is** that an organized classroom is free of chaos, and the teacher is basically stress-free. Which classroom would you choose?

---

# Procedure 2 for Teachers:
# Plan Well

### What Do They Do?

*Good teachers love to teach us*
*There is no doubt about it*
*They know just how to make a point*
*And never do they shout it.*
*They count the minutes till we come*
*And hate it when we leave*
*Teaching is their life, we're sure*
*From it there's no reprieve.*
*We wonder what they really do*
*When all of us go home*
*They must just wait around at school*
*Feeling so alone.*
*We're sure that they don't eat or sleep*
*Or shop or cook or sew*
*What do they do while we're at home?*
*We'd really like to know!*

*Elizabeth Breaux*

We plan for tomorrow! That's what we do. There truly is no reprieve. If we're not teaching, we're planning. We're not complaining; we really love what we do.

We are realistic. We know that the hard work is in the planning. When we plan a great lesson, the rest is fun! We can have a great time teaching.

We are never as effective when we wing it as we are when we have the lesson well planned. There are just no shortcuts. It's a given. We must plan for success.

## Tips for Planning Well

- Decide on your objectives. What is it that the students will know or be able to do at the end of this lesson?

- Plan your introduction. Make certain to tell the students what they will know or be able to do by the end of the lesson.

- Decide how you will "hook" the students. Don't skip this part. It is vital! We cannot reel them in until we hook them. It's that basic.

- Plan to model, model, and model. Show the students what they will be able to do by the end of the lesson. Let them see you do it. Have examples of other students' work available to share with them.

- Have several hands-on activities planned if possible. Mini-activities work best because they keep the lesson moving.

- Materials more than likely will be utilized during these activities. Have them organized and ready for use. (See Procedure 7 in Part II.)

- Have step-by-step directions ready to hand out to the students. (See Procedure 13 in Part II.)

- Plan to be an active participant in the lesson.

- Plan for early finishers. Don't allow idle time. If you do, you're asking for trouble.

- Plan your closure, making certain to allow enough time for it to be effective. Don't allow the bell to end your class.

## Classroom Scenario

There are two physical education teachers at this school. They teach at the same time and use the same gymnasium. Both are teaching bowling today. Unfortunately, one has planned well and one has not. Same grade level, same number of students, same everything. One lesson has been very well planned; however, the other one obviously has not. You'll have no trouble figuring out which is which in these examples.

*Coach Williams* obviously has done this before. Students enter the gym after "dressing out" for class and seem to know the procedure: sit in one's designated area while instructions are given. The bell rings, and Coach Williams is able to begin class immediately because all the students are seated and attentive.

Bowling pins have been set up, and lines have been drawn on the gym floor to mark the "lanes." The balls are on a rack at the top of the lanes. Small tables have been set up with two chairs at each one. Scorecards and pencils are on the tables.

Coach Williams calls for Group A to report to the area behind the pins, where each student takes a seat behind one of the lanes. She motions to Group B to be seated next to the bowling balls. She assigns Group C to the tables, and students in Group D are given jobs as "teacher assistants." These students serve as peer tutors would in the classroom. Their job is to critique the bowlers and assist them in improving their skills. Because they will be modeling for the bowlers, they get a chance to bowl too. Everyone is happy.

Coach Williams then directs all the students to watch what she is about to do. She walks over to the bowling balls and chooses one. She then moves to the lane, where she asks one of the teacher assistants to watch her as she practices her delivery, which she proceeds to execute. The delivery is awful! The ball skips two lanes and finally comes to rest against the back wall of the gym. (An observer would have to assume that Coach Williams has done this on purpose. Let's hope so.)

Everyone has a good laugh, and Coach Williams asks the teacher assistant to critique her form. This is hilarious, and the students really enjoy it. Now, after the teacher assistant has given the coach some pointers and modeled the correct form for her, the coach tries again. This time, of course, Coach Williams knocks down eight pins. (Nice try, Coach, but why not ten pins?) On her next delivery she knocks down the remaining two pins.

She then asks the scorekeepers, who are seated at the tables, to explain the procedure for scoring the two deliveries. With the coach's assistance they proceed to explain the scoring procedure. (A large laminated scorecard sits on a display easel next to the tables. Coach Williams writes the points on the card so that everyone can get a visual understanding of how the two shots are scored.)

Coach Williams explains that once all the students in the groups have taken their turns, the groups will rotate to another position. The students begin the activity, and it moves flawlessly for the remainder of the class period.

Approximately ten minutes before the bell rings Coach Williams blows her whistle, which is obviously the signal for all the students to stop and sit in their areas. She instructs those at the table to place all scorecards in the designated folders and take the scorecards for the next class out of their folders and place them on the tables. (This is her procedure for setting things up for the upcoming class.) She instructs those seated behind the bowling pins to set them up properly for the next class. She asks those who were bowling at the time to bring the bowling balls back to the rack. After closing the lesson, she instructs all the students to follow her to the dressing room to "dress in."

Have you noticed that the gym is completely set up and ready for the next class to begin and that Coach Williams had little to do with that . . . other than instructing the students to do it for her? What's even more impressive is that all this was done amid the utter chaos on the opposite side of the gym. What's going on there? Read ahead and you'll see.

*Coach James*, in contrast, got all the bad students again this year. It happens every year. Invariably! Coach Williams gets the good ones, and Coach James gets the bad ones. You know those students. They're late for class. They don't listen to instructions. They knock down the wrong pins. They throw the bowling balls at the other students instead of at the pins. They keep score in some kind of code that no one can decipher. They steal the pencils before they leave class. They even manage to steal a bowling ball or a bowling pin from time to time! (The coach still can't figure out that one.) They're awful creatures that no human being should ever have to teach.

Closer observation reveals that Coach James's lack of proper planning could have something to do with the chaotic scene. (Actually, that's putting it mildly. It has *everything* to do with it.) Nothing is in place. Bowling pins are scattered from the last class, and Coach James spends the beginning of this class period trying to put things back in order. (This, of course, allows the class to be out of order in the interim.) Groups are not preassigned. Instead, Coach James simply tells the students to get into groups. *Big mistake!* The scorecards for this class cannot be found because the students from the last class mixed them together with the cards from their own class. While Coach James is trying to separate the scorecards and put them into the proper folders, two students leave the gym to engage in a much more exiting activity somewhere else on campus. Two girls have just finished braiding each other's hair, and three others have just entered the gym from who knows where. Coach James seems oblivious to all this because she is so busy "fixing" things. And on and on and on.

---

**The fact is** that planning is everything. A well-planned lesson is much more likely to be a a well-taught lesson.

---

# Procedure 3 for Teachers:
# Reach Your Objectives

> Students must know what they will be able to do by the end of any lesson. It's really that simple. How well you teach them will determine whether the objectives are reached.

## Point to Ponder

When my mother taught me to tie my shoelaces, she probably said something like this: "Let's learn to tie your shoelaces." Then she started teaching! There were no "shoe-tying vocabulary words" or tiny "shoe-tying worksheets!" We didn't look up words in a dictionary or watch a video on shoe-tying. My mother knew that she didn't need any of that for this lesson to be taught effectively. (Besides, there were no videos back then.) Mama simply modeled the skill—several times, I'm sure—and then allowed me to try it, with her guidance, of course.

I knew, however, from the onset, that I was going to be able to tie my own shoes! That was the objective, plain and simple. I could see the light at the end of the shoe-tying tunnel. The lesson made sense. Everything that my mother was doing (explaining, modeling, assisting, guiding, critiquing) was a part of the "master" plan (the objective): *to teach me to tie my shoelaces.*

Notice that there were no fillers. My mother did not provide time for any shoe-tying busy work! We got right down to business, and I learned to tie my shoelaces in the most efficient way.

Admittedly, I did not reach a level of mastery on that first day of shoe-tying. In fact, my mother had to revisit the lesson from time to time over the course of the next few days, "reteaching" as needed until I no longer needed any help with the skill. I had mastered it!

*I am a right-handed person. My mother is left-handed. I did not realize until several years ago that I have always tied my shoes as a left-hander would. A friend of mine watched me tying my shoelaces one day and asked if I was left-handed. (Who notices those kinds of things, anyway? And who really cares?) The point is that we truly do learn from our teachers. Good or bad, they all teach us. My mother's objective was to teach me to tie my shoes in a certain way: the only way she knew. And she did. She taught me well. I probably have tied hundreds of thousands of shoes in my lifetime, and I've done it so well that I am a rare right-hander who ties her shoes left-handed. Good job, Ma!*

## Tips for Reaching Your Objectives

Ask yourself the following questions and then answer them:

- "What is it that I want my students to know or be able to do by the end of this lesson, and how will I relay this to the students so that they know exactly what they will learn or be able to do?"
- "Where will I display the objectives in the classroom so that all students can see them clearly upon entering the room?"
- How will I state the objective so that it is clearly understood by all the students?
- "How will I model the skill so that the objectives become even more concrete to the students?"
- "What is the most efficient 'real-life' method of teaching this skill that will ensure that all the students know what they need to do to meet the objectives?"
- "What activities will I plan for the students that will help them meet the objectives?"
- "Do the activities I have planned include several that are 'hands-on' in nature?"
- "Do my students know how to get help if they need it?"
- "How will I know if my students have met the objectives?"

It is critical that we first decide what the students should learn to do and then get down to the business of teaching. That's what we do in real life. We don't waste time on the fluff. We teach a skill well and then move on to another.

## Classroom Scenario

All the students at this school attend a "Computer Skills" class three times a week. The classes have been divided by levels of ability: Beginner, Intermediate, and Advanced. Let's take a look at two Beginners' classes. Same ability levels but two different teachers with two separate "agendas." Big difference.

Mrs. Get-In-There-and-Do-It (Mrs. G) is a "hands-on, real-life-approach" teacher. She knows that ultimately we all learn by doing. All that preliminary stuff is just that: stuff! She also knows that her students have minimal computer skills, a deficiency she is determined to rectify in the most efficient manner.

Written on the board in Mrs. G's room is the objective for the day: "All my students will be able to locate a specific website and then locate websites that provide similar information."

Mrs. G gets to work. There are desks in the room, but Mrs. G instructs all the students to sit at a computer instead. The computers have not been turned on, and so Mrs. G walks them through the process until all the computers are "booted up" and running.

Now Mrs. G shows the students how to hold the "mouse" in the palm of one's hand. She has them place their fingers on the right and left "clickers." She then instructs them to "roll" the mouse and notice how this "rolling motion" moves the pointer on the screen.

"Locate the Internet icon on the desktop," she says to the students. Then she explains to them that the desktop is what they see on the screen as they look for this icon. "An icon is a symbol of something," she says to them. "It represents a bigger picture."

Once all the students have located the Internet icon, she instructs them to point to it with the mouse. "Now," she says, "using your index finger (which is resting on the left clicker), click twice (double click) on the icon." The students follow her instructions and watch as the screen changes. "You have just entered the World Wide Web," she tells them. "The world is now at your fingertips!"

To make a long story short, Mrs. G teaches the students how to enter the web address that takes them to the predetermined website. She then teaches the students how to "search the web" for websites that will provide similar information. The students follow her directions and achieve the objectives for the day.

Mrs. G is not quite finished, however. She knows that she has just given her students a lot of information and wants to make certain that they all would be fairly comfortable performing this task on their own. "Okay," she says to them, "let's go through it one more time before the bell rings. The first thing I want all of you to do is to X-out." (Remember that many of them do not know the lingo yet.) "If you look at the top right-hand corner of your screen, you will see an X. Take your pointer and click on that X. Notice that you have returned to your desktop, which is where you were before we entered the Internet."

"Can someone tell me what we would do to reenter the Internet?" One student raises his hand and responds, "We would double click on the Internet icon." "Very good," replies Mrs. G. "Now everyone do it."

"Can someone tell me what we would do…" (She proceeds to take them through a complete review of the day's lesson.)

All the students have met the objectives in a minimal amount of time. Notice that there was no lecturing or note-taking involved in the lesson. Mrs. G knew that she had a skill to teach and simply got down to the business of teaching. She knew that her students were not familiar with computer terminology but that she could teach them the terminology through this "application format."

What is important here is that Mrs. G's students are "learning it by doing it" (as opposed to just "hearing about it," as you'll see in Mrs. Can't Do It Until We Learn It's class).

Mrs. Can't-Do-It-Until-We-Learn-It (Mrs. C) probably has some objectives somewhere in the back of her mind. Since they are so abstract, however, she does not see any reason to share them with her students. In her mind her objective is simply to "teach the students to use a computer." (A little vague.)

Mrs. C's students enter her class and are instructed to be seated at a desk. Computers line the walls of the room, but Mrs. C knows that these students do not know how to use a computer, so "why bother?" The students are given textbooks and instructed to open their notebooks. Mrs. C turns on the overhead projector so that all the students can see a list of computer terms that are unfamiliar and have no meaning to them. (Remember, they are "Beginners.") These are the terms that are listed:

| Desktop | Left-click | Website |
|---------|-----------|---------|
| Mouse | Pointer | Search engine |
| Right-click | Icon | X-out |

Mrs. C now instructs the students to use their textbooks to find the definitions of these terms. She tells them to write the terms, along with their definitions, in their notebooks. Once they have completed this "activity," they should read Chapter 1 in their textbooks. (Reading this chapter will, of course, provide additional "instruction" that may have been overlooked in the vocabulary "lesson.")

Question: What did Mrs. C's students learn today?

Answer: Nothing!

Remember that to learn, we must be able to make a connection. Mrs. C never connected these computer terms to the computer in any way. The terms might as well have been written in a foreign language. Assuming that Mrs. C's "objective" was to "teach students to use a computer," we can conclude that the objective was not met.

---

**The fact is** that if objectives are clear and concise (with a specific predetermined outcome of what the students will be able to do), teaching and learning take place. Remember that the objectives are not only for the students. They are used by the teacher to guide instruction.

---

# Procedure 4 for Teachers:
# Greet Your Students Every Day

### My Teacher Likes Me

*My teacher waits for us each day*
*And smiles to see us coming*
*She shakes our hands or pats our backs*
*(Her methods are quite cunning.)*
*"How are you?" she asks each one,*
*"So good to see you here."*
*"I read your paragraph last night,*
*Your words concise and clear."*
*"I really missed you yesterday,"*
*She says to yet another.*
*"Great work you did on Monday, Sam,*
*Can't wait to tell your mother."*
*I don't know how to thank her*
*Or if words can suffice*
*But I know as far as teachers go*
*I'd like to have her twice.*

*Elizabeth Breaux*

I'm not a big "statistics person," and so this is not based on any kind of survey, but I would estimate from my experience that at least 90% of any discipline problems that "could" occur in the typical classroom can be averted if the teacher simply greets the students at the door each day.

I'm warning you, however, that this greeting must be genuine. If it's not, the students will know it. It must be personal. Students must feel that you have made a personal connection with each of them. It doesn't need to be a long conversation-like exchange of words. If you read the poem above, you saw that the little "gestures" made by the teacher were very quick and simple. She did, however, manage to say something personal to the students.

It's hard not to respond to someone who smiles at you, calls you by your name, shakes your hand, and seems genuinely concerned about you. Think about it. It's human nature to respond positively to someone who treats you in a positive manner. (By the way, the reverse is also true.)

## Tips for Greeting Students Daily

- Make certain that your room is in order and ready so that you can be at your door as students begin arriving.
- Smile. If you don't feel like smiling, fake it! Students won't know. They'll just think you're happy. But fake it well because smiles must seem genuine too.
- If you're not comfortable with being spontaneous at first, think of a few "one-liners" you can rattle off as the students walk in. Make them personal. Once you've done this enough, it will become second nature. Here are some examples:
  - "Good morning, Sandra; nice to see you!"
  - "Nice haircut, Natasha!"
  - "Good game yesterday, Jim. You're a good basketball player!"
  - "Thanks, Marie, for helping your group yesterday. I appreciate that!"
  - "You're always smiling, Denise. You make me want to smile too!"
  - "I may need your help today, Cindy. Are you okay with that?"

If the teacher is making the students feel good about themselves, they will be more likely not to cause her or him any trouble or grief. It just won't occur to them. They like the teacher way too much!

## Classroom Scenario

Trouble is brewing on the playground. This "problem" has been going on for some time and finally is coming to a head. The two opposing "groups" approach each other. Words are exchanged, though fists are not raised. Word spreads quickly, and the crowds begin to gather. Teachers run to intervene. Thankfully, the bell rings. The teachers direct all the students to their classes. Tempers are flaring, but the students reluctantly move in the right direction. Mrs. Sun and Mrs. Moon, unaware of the situation that has just occurred, are in their classrooms awaiting the arrival of their students.

Mrs. Sun, upon the ringing of the bell, moves to the doorway to greet her students. As she watches them move down the hallway in her direction, she senses that something is wrong. She is aware that trouble has been about to surface on campus, and her "teacher's intuition" tells her that something bad has just happened. She arms herself with defusing words and goes to work.

"I need some help today, John. Can you sit behind my desk and wait for my directions?" "Sure," says John. "Good afternoon, Keisha. Awesome poem you wrote. Would you open your notebook and prepare to share it with the class?" "Jason, would you help Donna with the material that she missed yesterday when she was absent? Thanks so much!" And on and on until all the students have entered the room.

The bell rings, and Mrs. Sun closes the door. "Okay," says Mrs. Sun. "Everyone stop and look at me." (The students follow her directions.) "I want to thank you all for leaving the 'mess' on the playground and entering the class ready to work. I have sensed that something is going on between several students here on campus, and I am hoping that none of you would even consider involving yourselves in it. There will be no discussion about it or reference to it in this classroom, as we are far too mature for that. If you know someone who is involved in this mess, stay away from that person. I would be highly disappointed to learn that any of you have involved yourselves. I think highly of you all and don't want my opinion of you to be tainted. If you would like to talk to me about it later in private, please feel free to do so. Now, let's get to work."

Mission accomplished! Mrs. Sun, in her great wisdom, has defused another fire. Not only did she defuse it by diverting the students' attention as they entered her room, she took the opportunity to use it as a learning tool. If Mrs. Sun had not been waiting to greet her students, she might not have realized that she needed to arm herself. Because she greets her students daily anyway and has perfected the "art of manipulation," she is able to blindside the students without their realizing it. She calmed them down and gave them direction before the situation could develop any further. The students have no clue what just happened, but Mrs. Sun does—and she's shining now!

Mrs. Moon, in contrast, was still "rising" as the students began to enter her room. Many loitered outside the room, discussing the events that had just taken place. Many who had not witnessed the events were able to get the hot-off-the-press news from others while standing in the hallway. Opinions were shared, and the already fired tempers began emitting new flames. Raised voices alerted the students who had already entered the room to exit quickly to get a front-row seat for the "show." Mrs. Moon, sensing that something was amiss, finally made her way to the door. "Get in this room immediately," she screamed to the students. Some obeyed, and others ignored the command. Those who did obey brought the "outside" conversation back into the room, where it began to flare even more. "I said to get in the room," Mrs. Moon shouted. The principal, who happened to be entering the hallway, came to Mrs. Moon's assistance and settled the class. Several of the students had to be taken to the office, and the rest remained in class. Needless to say, not much effective instruction took place that day. Sadly, this could have been avoided if Mrs. Moon had been "on guard" at her doorway, where she would have been privy to this impending "situation."

**The fact is** that if we greet our students, they are more likely not to greet us with any surprises.

# Procedure 5 for Teachers:

# Encourage HOTS (Higher-Order Thinking Skills) in Your Students

### Higher-Order Thinking

*My teacher makes me think too much*
*He asks too many questions*
*Not the easy "yes" or "no" kind*
*His require expression.*
*And even if I answer right*
*He doesn't stop it there*
*He makes me answer "Why" or "How"*
*"What if?" "What then?" (who cares?).*
*He calls this "higher-order thinking"*
*(I'll tell him what I think.*
*On second thought, if I did that*
*My grades would surely sink.)*
*So I'll just play the game with him*
*I know it makes him happy*
*(But all this thinking makes me tired*
*I think I'll take a "nappy.")*

*Elizabeth Breaux*

Did you know that in the typical American school the majority of questioning in the classroom (through both written tests and general dialogue between the teacher and the students) occurs in a low-level, "spit-back of knowledge" type of format? Most of the time teachers simply "spit out" facts and then ask students to regurgitate those facts back to them. Some call it memorization. Some call it simple recall. Whatever you choose to call it, the fact is that it requires no critical thinking on the part of the students. Why do teachers continue to teach this way?

The truth is that many of us teach the way we were taught. We don't know a better way because we haven't seen a better way. If you are one of those teachers, this section is for you.

Think about the teacher you had in school who required that the students take a lot of notes. Do you remember? That's right. You remember because you recall all the studying and memorizing you had to do to pass the tests. Do you remember knowing in advance that if you memorized the notes, you could get an A? Because you were such a good student, you did memorize those notes, and you did get that A. What do you think would have happened, however, if in two weeks the teacher had given you the same test again? Yes, the same one, but this time the test was unannounced. If you were like 99% of the population, you probably would have failed the second test or scored much lower than you had on the first test. Why? Because you had not truly learned the material. You simply had memorized it for the test.

Memorization may have its place (a very small place, in my opinion), but its place is not in the world of the critical thinker. To think critically we must go far beyond the memorized facts, formulas, lists, dates, and the like. We must be able to take these facts, dates, and lists and apply them. To do that, we must be able to analyze, synthesize, and evaluate. Sheer memorization stops short of any of these higher-level skills.

## Tips for Encouraging Higher-Order Thinking

- ◆ Become familiar with the levels of thinking and questioning. (Go to any search engine and type in "Bloom's Taxonomy." You'll find plenty of information.)
- ◆ Take the information and evaluate your own test questions. (Do you ask mostly lower-level questions, or do you stimulate your students to think more critically?)
- ◆ Take the information and evaluate your own daily dialogue with your students. (Do you typically ask very direct questions that require a one- or two-word response, or do your questions stimulate critical thinking, thereby stimulating an ongoing dialogue between you and your students?)
- ◆ Make a list of words that you know are good "higher-order thinking" question starters and keep it handy, using it until you no longer need it. Here are some possible "start words":

| | |
|---|---|
| explain | rearrange |
| compare | infer |
| evaluate | conclude |
| what if? | change |
| why? | plan |
| design | separate |
| arrange | classify |

- Practice for a while and then ask a peer to come in and evaluate you.
- Take one of your tests and go through it. Place checks next to the questions that are higher-order/critical thinking questions.
- Go to your state's Department of Education website and search for released test items. Most states have "end of the year" tests that the students must pass. In some states students must pass these tests to proceed to the next grade. Your state's website probably is full of valuable information. Use it!

Enough talk. Let's look into the classrooms of two teachers. You'll recognize them both because they were your teachers way back when.

Mr. Knowledge can tell you the names of every president, every state, every country, every river, and every mountain range, along with the name of every student he has ever taught. He is so full of facts that his head has taken on the shape of an F. (Just kidding, but it sounded funny. I'm laughing right now.)

He is the universal lecturer. He can stuff more "stuff" into a one-hour class period than anyone I have ever known. He talks and talks, and his students write and write. Most bring along a tape recorder in case they miss something. The ironic thing is that students leave his class with a notebook full of stuff but a head that is basically empty. Why? Because they've learned nothing!

There is no dialogue between Mr. Knowledge and his students; therefore, there is no venue for encouraging higher-order thinking. His students are not mentally challenged, just physically exhausted.

Some of his students will go home and study—just as you did. Some will not bother. Those who study will pass the class. Those who don't will fail. This is the only thing that distinguishes one from the other, because the truth is that none of them have *learned* anything!

Mr. Knowledge often can be heard complaining in the teachers' lounge that "the kids fail because they don't study!" It sounds to me like Mr. Knowledge is saying that his students learn only from a notebook (if the lack of studying is what truly causes them to fail). I wonder if he realizes that this is what he is saying?

By the way, Mr. Knowledge's tests require no critical thought either. In fact, they are all formatted in the same way: Part I is a "Matching" section, and Part II is a "Fill-in-the-Blanks" section. There is one really good thing about this type of test, however: It's easy to grade and thus popular among the Mr. and Mrs. Knowledges of the school.

Let's move down the hallway and take a look into Mr. Analytical's classroom.

Mr. Analytical knows that learning occurs when we can take something into our lives and apply it. This is when the stuff takes on meaning. He knows that students must be able to relate all materials to their own lives in some way, and he knows that he is capable of helping them do that.

He believes that students must be made to think far beyond the written word. He also knows that this can happen only with his assistance. Mr. Analytical may ask a very basic, lower-level question from time to time, but he always follows it with a higher-level question to stimulate thought in his students and dialogue between himself and his students. Here is a typical conversation that would take place daily between Mr. Analytical and his students:

Mr. A:  "John, can you give me the answer to question 1?"

John:  "The answer is B."

Mr. A:  "Very good, John. You've been paying attention, but can you explain why answer A is incorrect?"

John:  "Because . . ."

Mr. A:  "Very good, John. Linda, how could you change the question so that C would be the correct answer?"

Mr. A makes his students think! He won't allow them simply to give an answer and move on. He forces them to explain, compare, analyze, synthesize, and so on.

A visitor to his classroom would be astounded at the constant dialogue that exists between Mr. A and his students because Mr. A constantly "forces" his students to think critically. Because he engages his students in a conversation, they have learned to engage both Mr. A and one another in these higher-order conversations. Mr. A is always questioning his students, and his students are questioning him. It's become second nature to all of them. It's part of the daily structure of the class.

Mr. A's written tests are also in a "higher-order-thinking" format. Here are some typical test questions that would appear on one of Mr. A's tests:

- Knowing what you already know about the supplies that Christopher Columbus had on his ship, compare them with the supplies a sailor today would use. What types of supplies would today's sailors use that would make the journey easier? What supplies today would be basically the same as those used during Columbus's time? Explain your reasoning.

- Using the map on page 12, give directions on how to get from Lafayette, LA, to Lockport, LA. Then draw a map of the school. Give directions on how to get from the cafeteria to the gymnasium.

- List the three branches of government. Then assign the three branches to three members of the school faculty. Explain why each one was assigned to this particular branch.

Mr. A's students invariably post some of the highest scores in the school on the end-of-the-year tests. Surprising? I think not.

---

**The fact is** that higher-order/critical thinking is stimulating. It stimulates thought and conversation. It encourages even the most "disengaged" students to engage. It promotes learning—real learning. Engage your students by using higher-order-thinking strategies. Your classroom will be a much more exciting place to live and learn.

---

# Procedure 6 for Teachers:
# Praise Every Single Positive Thing

### Thank Me

*My teacher says "thank you" for everything*
*For things you just wouldn't believe*
*So teachers, I'm sending a message to you*
*One I hope that you will retrieve.*
*If you thank me for the little things*
*Where "thank yous" are not expected*
*Then the bad things that I sometimes do*
*Will soon be redirected.*
*Some of us need you to notice us*
*Whether for good or for bad*
*And it seems the bad kids get your attention*
*That they otherwise wouldn't have.*
*So thank me for smiling and walking in line*
*Thank me for listening and being on time*
*Thank me for doing my work and you'll see*
*That I'll be the best kid, for you, I can be!*

*Elizabeth Breaux*

How often do you praise the positive things that are going on in your classroom? How often do you draw attention to the negatives?

Unfortunately, in the typical classroom far more positive things than negative things occur, yet teachers typically pay greater attention to the negative things at an alarmingly high rate.

I have a question for you: "What normally happens when you heap praise upon children for positive behavior?" Yes, you're right: They repeat the behavior, only this time they may do it a little better than they did the time before. It's a human response, by the way, that applies to everyone. When someone tells us that we've done a great job at something, we want to continue doing it. We seem to feel an innate obligation to continue making that person proud of us.

Think about one of your former teachers who really liked you. How did you know that this person liked you? Was it something the teacher did? Was it something the teacher said? Was it the way the teacher looked at you with approval? Or maybe it was the fact that the teacher talked positively about you to others. If you were really fortunate, the teacher talked one on one with you sometimes and even called your parents to tell them how terrific you were.

Now, think about the teacher you would prefer to forget. You know, the one who was a master at finding the negatives, the one who never said thank you. The one who never made mistakes but blamed the students for their shoddy work and unacceptable behavior.

*Which teacher would you like to be?*

## Tips for Accentuating the Positives

◆ First, sit down in a quiet space and make a list of the positive things you know happen daily in your classroom. Here are some examples of positives that we can (but too often don't) thank students for doing:

- walking into the classroom in an orderly manner
- saying "good morning" to you
- having all their materials
- being dressed according to the school's dress code
- raising their hands to speak
- doing their work
- helping someone else
- asking permission (for anything)
- volunteering to participate
- completing homework assignments
- improving their grades
- walking in line
- picking up trash

◆ Now circle the ones you regularly compliment.

◆ Develop a "plan of action" by circling three or four that you will address the very next day.

◆ Be persistent. Don't stop doing it. Add daily to the list of positives you will address.

## Classroom Scenario

Two sixth-grade classes, two sixth-grade teachers, both walking their classes from the cafeteria back to the classroom on the first day of school. Same time, same place, same behaviors (some good, some not so good) from the two classes. Different reactions from the two teachers, different responses from the two groups.

### Teacher A

"Thank you, thank you, thank you. This was awesome! Almost all of you followed the procedure exactly right on the first day of school. Wow! How did I get so lucky? This is going to be a great year! If you messed up, by the way, don't be so hard on yourself. You probably will get it right tomorrow. You may not be accustomed to walking in single file without talking for such a long distance. That's understandable. I'm so pleased that almost everyone got it right the first time. I feel like I've won the lottery! I can't wait to see all the other great surprises you all have in store for me."

### Teacher B

"Is it possible to make it all the way to the sixth grade and still not know how to walk in single file? How old do you need to be to be able to do that? Am I going to have to fuss about this every day? This is ridiculous! Is this really a sixth-grade class? It seems more like third grade, but even most of them know how to walk in line. Now hurry up. Let's get to class. We've got plenty to do today, and we've already wasted time!"

---

**The fact is** that if we want positive responses from our students, we must be positive ourselves. The only way to reinforce the positives is to accentuate them. The best way to reinforce the negatives is to accentuate them. *Be positive!*

---

# Procedure 7 for Teachers:

# Teach with Enthusiasm Using a Real-Life, Hands-on Approach

## Be Happy, Happy, Happy

*My teacher talks and talks and talks, we write and write and write*

*Sometimes I'd like to say to her, "Excite, excite, excite!"*

*There's no inflection in her voice—no happy, happy, happy*

*Just lots of "Hurry, get this done; be snappy, snappy, snappy."*

*We work and work and work some more, then bring home more to do*

*We're busy, busy, busy, and we still don't have a clue*

*You see, my teacher, if you'd let us try it, try it, try it*

*You'd be proud when most of us would buy it, buy it, buy it!*

*Elizabeth Breaux*

Humor me for a minute. Go back and look at the title of this section. What do you think? A little long for a title? Encompasses too much for one section? I thought the same thing at first.

Initially this was intended to be two separate sections: "Teaching with Enthusiasm" and "Using a Real-Life, Hands-on Approach." When I began writing, however, it became apparent that the two are so closely related that they need to be conjoined. So here it is. Once you read and think about it, I'm sure you'll agree with me on this one. When we teach a lesson using a real-life, hands-on approach, it's difficult not to be enthusiastic. It's so much fun. The students love it, we love it, and life is wonderful! Have you ever watched or taught a lesson that was hands-on, real-life? If you have, you've noticed the same thing that I have: All the students are on task, are engaged in the lesson, and are having so much fun that they don't realize how much they are learning! Is this not what teaching and learning are all about? And the greatest perk of all is that the teacher is having fun too. It's "life come full circle" in the classroom! Everyone's engaged, everyone's happy, everyone's learning, and life is beautiful. (Maybe I'm exaggerating, but it really can be this good. Try it!)

First, realize that the following teaching methods are not considered effective methods of instruction. This is not to say that they are not used sporadically in the classroom, but the operative word is "sporadically."

- *Lecture.* This is still one of the most frequently used teaching methods, even though it is extremely ineffective. Think about the teachers we had who stood in the front of the classroom, often behind a lectern or desk, and talked in a monotone, mundane, unenthusiastic manner for hours on end. How bored were we? How much did we learn? How much would we have paid to avoid that classroom each and every day? The teaching method just described is called lecturing, and it's extremely nonengaging.

I also remember the teacher who loved to talk "to" us as opposed to "at" us. She had a way of telling a story in which everything was related to our lives in some way. She paid special attention to making certain that all the students were able to share their experiences throughout the lesson. We created things, both literally and figuratively, that gave meaning to the lesson. Yes, she talked to us a lot but never lectured at us.

- *Note-Taking.* Don't get me wrong. I'm not opposed to having students jot down some notes from time to time as long as the notes have a meaning based on prior knowledge. (In fact, there are some really effective, highly engaging note-taking strategies out there.) What I am opposed to, however, is note taking in the absence of teaching.

Consider an effective note-taking scenario in which the teacher teaches a history lesson through storytelling. The "characters"/historians in the story are related to the students' lives in some way. After the students have an understanding of the events in history, asking them to take a few notes actually gives meaning to the note-taking. The students already have made sense of what is being written, and so the note-taking is not viewed as another meaningless, time-consuming task.

Remember the class where you walked in and the teacher had several pages of notes for you to copy? (I believe the teacher even called it a "study guide.") You spent hours taking notes and then spent even more hours studying notes that had no meaning because the material was never taught to you. This was the same teacher who said, "Kids today fail because they don't study!" Where's the teaching? (How would you like to go to a workshop or seminar at which the speaker gives you pages of notes to copy and study while teaching nothing?)

◆ *Silent Reading with Little or No Guidance.* Before you throw this book against the nearest wall, let me assure you that I am not opposed to reading. I was a language arts teacher. I love to read and to see my students engaged in a good book. However, I, like you, remember the teacher who said, "Open your book to page 30, read the story, and then answer the questions at the end of the story."

I also remember the teacher who actually taught while the story was being read. Sure, we read silently, or aloud, or in groups, but we learned about story elements through discussions along the way. We learned vocabulary by stopping when we came across unfamiliar words and using context clues or other real-life strategies to help us determine their meaning. We compared the story with events in our own lives or with a previously read story. We learned about characterization and stopped midway into the story to write a character sketch. It might have taken an entire week to read that story, but we learned so much along the way!

◆ *Testing.* Yes, we've got to assess our students. Don't forget, however, that the test is not exclusively for the students; it's for the teacher too. (See Procedure 18 in Part II.) It's one of the ways we teachers determine whether the students are learning what we've taught. The test allows us to determine whether reteaching is necessary. Give that test and get right back to teaching!

◆ *Worksheets.* I am not opposed to worksheets either, as long as they are used sparingly. Remember that a worksheet is used for one of two reasons: as a mini-assessment of what has been taught and/or as extra practice for or reinforcement of what has been taught. We all remember the teacher who monopolized the copy machine. The one who copied stacks of worksheets every week. The one who gave you a packet of worksheets (busy work) almost every day. The one who sat at her desk grading yesterday's packet of worksheets while you worked on today's packet. The one who had tomorrow's packet of worksheets ready for today's early finishers. Remember?

## Tips for Using a Real-Life, Hands-on Approach

◆ Remember that you are the teacher. Everything else is just supplementary.

◆ Relate all lessons to real life.

◆ Tell stories that engage students in the lesson. The stories can be true or fabricated. The students will respond regardless!

- Create "manipulatives" to accompany lessons. These hands-on, task-oriented activities always engage students.

- Create stations in your room where groups of students can work on different activities at their own pace.

- Work "with" the students. If they see that you are actively engaged in what they are doing, they will view the activity as being meaningful.

- Observe successful colleagues whenever possible—with their permission and the permission of your administrator, of course. You'll be amazed at the wonderful activities that go on in many classrooms.

## Classroom Scenario

In this school all reading teachers followed the same weekly curriculum at each grade level. The sixth-grade teachers were to teach "story elements" to their classes during this particular week. What you will find below is a perfect example of how different teaching techniques can foster incredibly different results.

### Mrs. Pepper

Mrs. Pepper loves teaching. She is always on her feet concocting some new idea for engaging her students, and she had a great idea for this week's lesson.

When the students entered her classroom on Monday, they received a packet of color-coded 3-by-5 cards. They also received a color-coded chart that coincided with the cards. The teacher began by telling the students exactly what the lesson would and would not entail. She invited them to sit back and relax as they listened to her stories and jot down a few notes on their cards, which they could use later as "crutches."

That teacher told one of the most engaging stories I have ever heard. The story was about the many perils of one of her former students who once had decided to lie about his homework. Since one lie, of course, breeds another, the story included details on what ensued for this "main character." As the teacher reached the "climactic moment" of the story, all the students were literally on the edges of their seats.

Then Mrs. Pepper began teaching the actual elements of a story. She discussed with the students the meanings of such elements as setting, characters, conflict, climax, resolution, and theme. As they discussed those elements, the students jotted down a few notes on their color-coded cards, which the teacher again referred to as their crutches. (Remember that the colors on the cards coincided with the colors on the desk charts.)

Once all the story elements had been discussed and real-life experiences had been shared by all, the teacher told another "true" story. Upon the completion of that story, the students were given story element strips. Each strip included an actual element from the story that had just been told. The students had to lay the strips on the charts next to the correct story elements. They were encouraged to use their crutches (the color-coded cards) if they could not remember the definition of a particular element. The teacher then told the students that they would be allowed to use the crutches for future stories, also assuring them that very soon they would not need them. (This is the point where the teacher knows that true learning has taken place.)

This was one of the most exciting lessons I have ever seen. The teacher was extremely enthusiastic, and her enthusiasm was infectious. All the students were engaged, were sharing experiences, and were grasping the concept. Wow!

On to Mrs. Cucumber's room. Same objectives, same subject matter, same grade level. Different teaching methods. Different results? You decide.

## Mrs. Cucumber

Mrs. Cucumber has never been known as an enthusiast. On the contrary, she is the opposite. She spends very little time planning and wouldn't know an innovative, hands-on, real-life teaching strategy if it peeled her and ate her for lunch.

Students enter Mrs. Cucumber's room and are told to take out their notebooks. All the story elements are written on the board, along with a short definition of each one. An observer notices that listed on another board are today's "activities." Activity 1 states, "Copy the story elements along with their definitions into your notebooks." The students then get to work on their note-taking as Mrs. Cucumber does something that requires that she stay seated at her desk.

Some students finish quickly, as will happen in any classroom, whereas others are far behind. The early finishers, of course, have nothing to do and begin engaging in off-limits activities that require constant redirecting from Mrs. Cucumber. (All accomplished in the "seated at her desk" position, of course.)

After several power struggles ensue between Mrs. Cucumber and some of the early finishers, Mrs. Cucumber decides to suggest that the early finishers begin working on Activity 2 on the "assignment" board, which states, "Read the story in your text on page 38." Some students begin reading after several of the disgruntled groan and grumble at the suggestion. (Mrs. Cucumber stretches out her legs while still in the seated position.)

An observer then notices what you probably have guessed already: Activity 3 on the board instructs students to complete the worksheets on "story elements" once the story has been read.

Here are two questions for you to consider:

- When did instruction take place?
- How much have the students learned about story elements?

**The fact is** that if you're a Mrs. Cucumber, your students will pickle you! If you want your students to learn the material, you must teach it by using a real-life, hands-on approach. You, the teacher, must be a model of enthusiasm if you want your students to display an enthusiastic approach to learning in your classroom. Material with no meaning is simply material. We must make that material come to life in our classrooms. We have the power to kill it or to bring it to life for our students. Please don't be the teacher who smothers those sparks. Instead, be the one who ignites them.

# Procedure 8 for Teachers:
# Approach Every Situation Proactively

### Help Me!

*I'm repairing one as another one breaks*
*His problem's contained, but hers escapes*
*This fire's extinguished, while that one bakes*
*Help me, please, for my sanity's sake!*

                    *Elizabeth Breaux*

## Are you a "Proactive" or a "Reactive" Teacher?

**Proactive** teachers seem to have less stress in their lives, and their classes seem to run smoothly.

- They are very organized.
- They greet students daily.
- They have a lot of procedures and are masters at implementing them consistently.
- They compliment students constantly.
- They accentuate the positives—they thank students!
- They make positive home contacts soon.
- They are masters at getting students on their side.
- They apologize when they make "mistakes."
- They are consistent and fair and firm but kind.
- They teach with enthusiasm and always "appear" to love what they do.

**Reactive** teachers spend a lot of their time trying to "fix" things.

- They are disorganized.
- They do not greet students at the doorway.
- They may have procedures, but they don't implement them consistently.

- They rarely compliment students.
- They rarely thank students.
- They seldom, if ever, make positive home contacts.
- They tend to alienate students.
- They never apologize because they don't make mistakes.
- They are inconsistent and therefore appear to be unfair and/or unkind.
- They rarely smile and are obviously unhappy in their chosen profession.

## Tips for Becoming More Proactive

- Study the characteristics of proactive teachers.
- Evaluate yourself. In which areas are you proficient, and in which areas are you lacking?
- If you're really brave, have a peer who knows you well evaluate you. Tell that person to *be honest, pull out all the stops,* and *let you have it* if necessary. Listen to the evaluation. Remember that sometimes we need to step back from a situation and look at it through someone else's eyes. That's not always easy to do, and so you should have someone else's eyes do it for you.
- Start working to improve the areas where you have determined that work is needed.

## Classroom Scenario

It's the third week of school. The principal has given all the teachers two weeks to implement and practice procedures in their classrooms. Classroom observations begin. Here's what the principal observes.

### Mrs. Proactive

As the principal enters the sixth-grade hallway, she is drawn immediately to the classroom of Mrs. Proactive. Mrs. Proactive is standing at her doorway greeting her sixth-graders as they enter the room. Her infectious smile and cheery demeanor seem to beckon the students to come in and enjoy the day. A simple "good morning" would suffice for most, but Mrs. Proactive doesn't stop at that. "Nice to see you, today, Laurie," she says. "I really missed you yesterday." "How's your mother doing since the accident?" she asks Jonathan. "Great job on your test, James. I'm so proud of you. Keep it up!"

Once all the students have entered the room, Mrs. Proactive steps in and enthusiastically compliments the entire class for walking in quietly and seating themselves. "I can't imagine having a better group of students," she says to them. "And thank you for picking up your notebooks from the counter and preparing them for the day. You all surely do catch on quickly!"

At this point it is obvious that Mrs. Proactive has the students on her side and eating out of her hand. It seems that they want to do everything they can to please her.

Mrs. Proactive then sets her timer for three minutes and instructs the students to complete the bell-work assignment quickly. (See Procedure 3 in Part II for more on this.) All the students commence working until the timer buzzes. Mrs. Proactive then has them share the work they have just completed.

"We will now move into our groups for our cooperative reading session," says Mrs. Proactive. "On the sound of three, all students will follow the procedure for getting into groups." (See Procedure 13 in Part II.) "You have thirty seconds. One . . . two . . . three . . . go!" The students move quickly but in an orderly way into their groups and wait for further instructions from Mrs. Proactive.

The rest of the class period runs just as smoothly. Procedures are obviously in place and are strictly enforced. Mrs. Proactive approaches everything with a smile and a compliment, averting any bad behaviors and avoiding confrontations. She even disciplines with a smile by first telling the students what they are doing well and then gently insisting that they correct what needs correcting. They just do it, and always with a smile. They are giving back exactly what they are getting from Mrs. Proactive.

Mrs. Proactive's class runs like clockwork. Even the "noise" is structured and nonchaotic. Group work has the potential for getting out of control, but not in Mrs. Proactive's classroom.

Needless to say, Mrs. Proactive seldom has any discipline problems. Her students are productive. Their test scores are consistently among the highest in the school, and she has very little work-related stress. Does it get any better than this?

Now on to Mrs. Reactive's room. Remember that all the teachers have had two weeks to implement and practice their procedures.

## Mrs. Reactive

The bell rings, and the principal moves in the direction of Mrs. Reactive's room. He notices that Mrs. Reactive is not standing at her doorway. The students, however, are loitering outside her classroom. The bell rings, and many are still not in class. A few seconds pass, and several of the students begin making their way into the room. As the principal nears the doorway of the classroom, he hears the confrontation that takes place between Mrs. Reactive and the students who were tardy. "Where have you been?" asks Mrs. Reactive. (*Big mistake.* Don't ask students a question unless you truly want an answer. In this case Mrs. R knows exactly where they've been, but she has given them a chance to "explain.") "My teacher kept me late," answers one student. "Which teacher is that?" asks Mrs. R. "My gym teacher," the student says. "You didn't even have gym class last period," screams Mrs. R. "Oh, yes, I did," the student answers. "They changed my schedule." Mrs. R has set the stage for chaos. Instead of extinguishing the fire, she has added fuel to it. Actually, she was arguably the one who was responsible for starting the fire in the first place!

The principal notices that several students are roaming around the classroom. Mrs. R demands that all be seated, but few listen. Some inch their way toward their seats but are obviously not in a hurry. "Did you hear me?" screams Mrs. R. "No," answers one of the students. "Can you say it a little louder?" "That was very disrespectful," Mrs. R exclaims. "I do not allow students to disrespect me. Now shut up and get out your notebooks!"

The principal observes that most of the students eventually take out their notebooks but are in no hurry to get to the task at hand. Mrs. R. then refers the students to the list on the chalkboard. The list reads as follows:

Read the story on pages 13–28.

Copy the questions at the end of the story.

Answer the questions at the end of the story.

Complete the vocabulary assignment.

Complete any unfinished work as homework.

After several minutes of mumbling and grumbling the students reluctantly begin to work. Mrs. R. is now seated behind her desk, where she remains for the duration of the class period.

The principal, who has the option of leaving the room (an option that the students do not have), returns to his office. Thirty minutes later four students come to him with discipline referrals. Guess which teacher sent them.

---

**The fact is** that we have the option of being proactive or reactive teachers. We truly can set ourselves up for success so that we do not have to put out fires constantly. It takes hard work, dedication, planning, consistency, and follow-through. Are you up to the challenge?

---

# Procedure 9 for Teachers:
# Maintain Your Composure

### On the Edge

*The blood is bubbling in my toes*
*Meandering up my legs it goes*
*Into my stomach, hear it roar*
*Approaching my neck, I feel it soar*
*My face is red, my veins stick out*
*I'm certain I'm about to shout*
*With one deep breath and one long sigh*
*I smile real big and stifle the cry!*

*Elizabeth Breaux*

Is this a tough one or what? It's one that takes practice, especially if you're not a natural at maintaining your composure. Some people are, and don't you just hate them? You know the ones. They keep their cool no matter what. Don't you just want to see them sweat? Just once? Hear them scream? Just once? See the veins in their temples bulge? Just once?

As professionals we must maintain our composure at all times. We have no choice! We are role models for our students. Consider the following:

- If I scream at my students, I am modeling screaming!
- If I roll my eyes at a student, I am modeling the disrespectful eye-rolling technique we all detest.
- If I react with sarcasm, I am modeling sarcastic behavior for my students.

I am not an administrator and have no intention of ever becoming one. If I were to become one, however, I would implement a "no screaming" policy on my campus. There's just no room for it. There are no exceptions either. It simply would not be allowed. Students have enough chaos in their lives. All students, even the really irritating ones, need to trust in the solace of a calm, caring environment when they are at school.

How apt are you to listen to someone who screams at and belittles you? Not only would you not listen, you would seek revenge! It might not be immediate, either. In fact, it might be slow, insidious, and painful. Don't set yourself up for this by screaming at and belittling students. It doesn't matter whether you think they deserve it. *No one deserves it.*

When you lose it in front of your students, you are modeling that behavior, plain and simple. Don't even give yourself the option. Just don't do it!

## Tips for Maintaining Your Composure

- Start by making a promise to your students at the beginning of the year. (I did this every year.) Promise your students that you will never raise your voice to them no matter what unless their lives are in danger and screaming is warranted. I really did this every single year on the first day of school. I told them that not only would I never raise my voice to them, I expected them to treat me and their classmates with the same respect.

- Tape yourself. No kidding! It's an awesome self-evaluating tool. You may not believe that it's you whom you are watching. I did this at the suggestion of one of my peers many years ago, and I found out so much about myself, including some things that I didn't really want to know but was happy to discover.

- When you are about to reprimand a child for anything, start by saying something positive to the student. This completely defuses students, and the situation doesn't have a chance to escalate.

- When you feel that you are about to explode, leave the situation alone for a while. Tell the student that you are really upset and that if you deal with the situation at that moment, you may say or do something unprofessional. Tell the student to give you some time to think about it and you will get back to him or her. This serves a dual purpose in that it gives both you and the student much-needed "cool-down" time.

## Classroom Scenario

It's been a long day, and it's still morning. The bell rings, and you are heading toward your classroom when a young lady comes flying out of a classroom and almost knocks you over. She does not stop to consider excusing herself or apologizing in any way. She is obviously in a hurry. You notice that her shirt is not tucked in her pants, her shoes are off (she's in her socks), and she's chewing gum. You are perceptive enough to know that this is not an emergency situation, and that infuriates you even more. How will you handle this in a professional manner, making certain to maintain your composure?

Let's look at how Mrs. Professional would handle it and then, of course, at how Mrs. Unprofessional would handle it.

### Mrs. Professional

Mrs. Professional takes a deep breath, puts a big smile on her face, and summons the young lady to her. The young lady, who is certain she is in really big trouble, turns abruptly (a real test of Mrs. Professional's ability to maintain her composure) and returns to where Mrs. P is standing. Mrs. P puts her hand on the young lady's shoulder and says, "First, let me tell you that you are as cute as can be! Did you have a sister who went to school here?" The young lady, who was prepared to be defensive, puts a big smile on her face and begins a friendly conversation with Mrs. P about her sister. Now that Mrs. P has made certain to compose herself and to ensure that the young lady will not become defensive, she says to her, "Okay, I want you to read my mind." (Mrs. P, smiling, gives the young lady a few seconds to think about that one.) The young lady responds, "I know, my shirt is not tucked in and my shoes are off, but I was in my dance class." Mrs. P responds, "Oh, well, that explains it, but what about the gum you are chewing? That is *never* allowed. Would you quickly throw it in the garbage can so that I can remember you as the cooperative young lady you seem to be?" The young lady, still with a big smile on her face, says "Yes, ma'am." She turns, holds the door for Mrs. P to enter the office area, and tells Mrs. P to have a nice day.

Before you read about Mrs. Unprofessional, I want you to think about all the things Mrs. P could have done to infuse, as opposed to defuse, this situation. That's what Mrs. U did, and did it blow up in her face! Read on if you dare.

### Mrs. Unprofessional

Mrs. Unprofessional can take no more. That was the last straw. Her blood has boiled and her veins are exploding, and it's all the fault of this young lady. "Come here," she screams at the top of her lungs. The young lady turns and slowly makes her way back to Mrs. U "Hurry up! I don't have all day to wait for you." The young lady rolls her eyes and pops her gum. (Another vein bulges in Mrs. U's neck.) "Do you realize that you almost knocked me down? Answer me! I can't hear you." The young lady replies in a very sarcastic tone, "If I had wanted to knock you down, I would have. I saw you and I didn't knock you down, so what are you hollering about?" "Get to the office right now, young lady," screams Mrs. U. "Who do you think you are, talking to me like that? I am writing you up, and they'd better send you home. This is ridiculous."

This "conversation" now moves into the office area. Mrs. U immediately begins filling out an office referral/discipline form, and the back-and-forth confrontation continues. Mrs. U has so much to write that an additional sheet has to be attached to the form.

---

**The fact is** that although students should *never* be allowed to be disrespectful to teachers, teachers have the obligation to handle situations in a professional manner in which they do not induce students to become disrespectful. We always have a choice when handling a potentially dangerous situation: We can infuse the fire with fuel, or we can put it out. The latter is a win-win situation. Kids will be kids, but adults must remain adults. The bottom line in the situation described above is that the best results were achieved by the more professional teacher.

---

# Procedure 10 for Teachers:
# Be a Role Model

## I Heard What You Did

*If I can just remember*
*That my words are simply sounds*
*That children hear in one ear and out*
*Too often, I have found*
*And more compared to what I do*
*(Or less to be exact)*
*For what I do is what they hear*
*This matter is a fact*
*Children watch our every move*
*It's what we do, not say*
*That children mimic every time*
*The power's in the play.*

*Elizabeth Breaux*

"Don't *tell* me what to do, *show* me! Don't tell me to get organized if you are disorganized! Don't tell me to be on time if you are often late! Don't tell me not to raise my voice to others if you raise your voice to others!"

As teachers, we know the importance of teaching certain life skills to our students, and we are masters at telling them what to do and how it should be done. We often forget, however, that we must be role models. One slip-up and they've got us! They really do. They know we're about to mess up before we know it. They're waiting for it. It's fun for them!

This is not done consciously, by the way. It's intuitive. People at all age levels judge one another by the actions they exhibit instead of the words they use. People don't hear what we say nearly as clearly as they hear what we do!

Whether we like it or not, teachers are constantly under scrutiny. We may be the most important role models in the lives of many of the children we teach. We have no choice but to become masters at this craft. We accepted this when we applied for this job and said, "Pick me, pick me. I'll be the best teacher I can possibly be!"

Many years ago I began doing the "1, 2, or 3" exercise with my students. I came up with this idea in an attempt to have students evaluate themselves according to the following criteria:

*1s are those who do the wrong thing even if they are being watched.*

*2s are those who do the right thing, but only if they are being watched.*

*3s are those who do the right thing even if they are not being watched.*

I would ask students to place themselves in one of the categories. (This was private, of course, not to be shared with others.) Then we would discuss our goal, which was, of course, to "be a 3." From that day forward, if I ever needed to step outside the room to talk to someone, I simply stood in front of the class and gave the hand signal: the three fingers. The message was clear, and the students knew exactly what was expected.

It wasn't until several years later that my sister, Annette, came up with the idea of using this concept in the presentations we do for teachers. It made perfect sense. If students fall into the categories of 1s, 2s, and 3s, so do teachers. "You see," Annette says to our audiences, "we cannot expect our students to be 3s if we are not 3s ourselves!" How powerful is that?

## Tips for Being a Role Model

◆ Make a list of the characteristics that you want to see displayed in your students. Your list most likely will resemble this one:
  • is self-motivated
  • is organized
  • is polite
  • turns in assignments on time
  • takes criticism well
  • does not instigate trouble
  • never raises his or her voice to others
  • does not procrastinate
  • is punctual
  • is friendly
  • does not overreact
  • works well with others

- is willing to compromise
- has high expectations for himself or herself
- goes above and beyond what is expected

◆ Now take that list and write your name at the top. Do it now! Don't procrastinate or overreact (just kidding). Seriously, we *must* be models of all we want our students to be—*all the time*. So go ahead and write your name on the list and evaluate yourself. Are you a 1, a 2, or a 3? Remember that as role models we must be 3s all the time. We have no choice. It's our mission as molders of young lives and young minds.

◆ Now take your list and start practicing. Some of these things may come easily and naturally to you, but some will not. That's all right. Start practicing anyway. Become aware of your actions toward and reactions with students. This is an awesome opportunity to grow. If you are really a brave soul, post the list on your classroom wall for all to see. Tell your students that these are the things you expect of them and also of yourself. Have them keep you honest! They will. They'll love it. And they'll respect you for being so real with them. Everyone wins!

## Classroom Scenario

Mrs. Nurture and Mrs. Slaughter have both been teaching at this elementary school for over twenty years. They both teach fifth grade, and their classrooms are adjacent to each other. Ironically, however, and to the dismay of Mrs. Slaughter, Mrs. Nurture—by chance of course—gets all the "good kids" every year. This, of course, leaves the rest of the fifth-graders (the bad ones) for Mrs. Slaughter. Is Mrs. Slaughter simply a magnet for bad luck, or is something else going on here? You decide.

### Ms. Nurture

Ms. Nurture greets her students and everyone else she meets with a smile. She always appears to be happy. Ms. Nurture has a vision and an outline for the structure of her classroom, and she seldom deviates from them. Her students know what to expect from her and know what she expects from them. She compliments her students constantly and is a master at finding the positives in them. Her students are ultimately successful and truly enjoy and appreciate the pleasant learning environment she has created for them.

Fellow teachers love Ms. Nurture because she is always kind and always real. She can be trusted as both a mentor and a friend. She is not a gossiper and would never even entertain the idea of having a conversation that was not a positive one. She always seems to find the good in everyone. Everyone wants to be more like Ms. Nurture.

The administration loves and respects Ms. Nurture for the same reasons. They particularly appreciate the fact that she takes care of business in her own classroom and rarely sends the problems to them. She is impeccable in her paperwork, always on time in turning in the abundance of forms that are due in the office, and always ready to lend her assistance (in her "free time," of course) whenever needed. She never complains about anything, although she is not afraid to approach the administration to discuss a problem and offer a solution. The administration prays daily for every teacher to be "more like Ms. Nurture."

## Ms. Slaughter

Ms. Slaughter, in contrast, is an obviously unhappy person. It's not her fault, however. Remember that she is the one who gets all the "bad kids" every year!

Ms. Slaughter never greets students. (This is probably because she is late for class herself or is trying to return the classroom to some semblance of order.) She often is heard saying that she would "find the positives in her students if only they would give her something to find." (She obviously doesn't get it.)

Ms. Slaughter is known by all as a screamer, but let's face it, she has to scream. "It's the only way the students will listen to me," she says. Her students, of course, are very disrespectful to her and often can be heard screaming back at her. That's all right, though, because it gives Ms. Slaughter license to scream even more.

Ms. Slaughter doesn't spend much time planning but can be seen and heard quite clearly in the lounge on a daily basis. She always has a story. You know the kinds of stories she tells because you probably have several "Ms. Slaughters" on your faculty: "Children today—no respect, no self-motivation, and so *unfriendly!*"

Ms. Slaughter obviously has a lot of problems: problems with students, problems with parents, problems with peers, problems with the administration, and on and on. What Ms. Slaughter probably has never considered is that *she may be part of the problem.* Until she has this revelation, she will never empower herself to be part of the solution.

**The fact is** that we are constant role models for our students and our peers. People truly see what we do before they hear what we say. Don't ever model a behavior that you would not want to see displayed in your students. It's that simple. Please don't "Slaughter" your students.

# Part II

# Procedures for Teachers and Their Students

In Part II of this book you will learn how to *teach*, *practice*, and *implement* procedures in the classroom. One of the worst mistakes we make as teachers is to assume that the students already know our procedures. If we make this incorrect assumption, we are laying the groundwork for failure.

Instead, place your students at ease from day 1. Tell them that there are many procedures that they will be expected to follow and that you will teach them each procedure one at a time, practicing it with them. Also, take the fear of failure away by letting them know that you do not expect them to implement the procedures properly in the initial stages but will remind them when they "mess up" and allow time for more practice.

In Part II you will find twenty-five procedures made easy. For each procedure, suggestions are provided for "How to Teach It," "How to Practice It," and "How to Implement It." Begin teaching procedures immediately. Do not waste time. Procedures are the foundation for the rest of your year. Do not take this lightly! Remember, however, that procedures will work only if they are implemented properly. Proper implementation is the job of the teacher! If we don't implement the procedures, guess who will implement them for us? That's correct: *the students*.

It is important to note here that there are no sections in this book that specifically address "rules and consequences." This is intentional in that the book deals strictly with "procedures." This is not to say, however, that rules and consequences are not a vital part of the structure of every classroom. They certainly are. A well-managed classroom, however, has many procedures and only a few rules. There is one distinct difference between rules and procedures: Rules have consequences, but procedures do not; they are simply "practiced to perfection." In my experience, procedures (if practiced to perfection) virtually eliminate the need for so many rules.

# Procedure 1
## for Teachers and Their Students:
# Entering the Classroom

Want to know what kind of teaching is going on inside a classroom? Simply watch the students enter that classroom. The manner in which students enter a teacher's classroom is an immediate indication of the type of learning environment that exists in that classroom. A classroom where students enter in an orderly fashion is a classroom where teaching and learning take place in an orderly fashion.

## How to Teach It

Tell the students that the manner in which they enter the classroom often sets the tone for their success during the class period. Tell them that people usually base assumptions about students' character on the way the students conduct themselves and that you, their teacher, want to assume only the best about them. Tell them that you expect them to enter your classroom in an orderly fashion, on time. (See Procedure 2 in Part II.) Tell them that you expect them to go immediately to their seats and prepare for class. Let them know that bell work (see Procedure 3 in in Part II) should begin immediately, without instructions from the teacher.

The teacher should model this for the students. Have fun with this! The students love it. Show them the incorrect way first. No holds barred; let out all the stops! Become the great actor you have always wanted to be and let them see you as you mimic their unruly friends—the friends who do it the wrong way and are always in trouble. The students love this part, and you get to make your point.

Then get serious. Let them know that what they just witnessed is what you never want to witness in them. Model the correct way now. It's not as much fun, but you'll get to have fun again when you model the rest of the procedures.

## How to Practice It

First, ask for three volunteers who would like to attempt the procedure. Allow them to attempt or model the procedure, both correctly and incorrectly, for the class. Allow the class to distinguish between the correct and incorrect examples.

Tell the students that they are going to practice entering the room. Remind them of what is expected and then allow them to exit the room quietly. Have them line up in the hallway and prepare to pretend that they are coming into the classroom for the first time today. (Don't forget to have them bring all their books with them. You want this practice session to be as authentic as possible.)

Now, instruct them to enter the room. As they enter, watch their every move. Compliment those who follow the procedure correctly but do not chastise those who do not. Remember that some are going to "mess up" for whatever reason. Don't worry about that. Just practice again, remembering to shower the words "thank you" on those who do it properly. The others will follow their lead when they realize that you are serious about this. After a couple of practice sessions thank them profusely for their cooperation and remind them that they should begin implementing this procedure the next time they enter the classroom.

## How to Implement It

Implementation comes with the expectation that students will do this correctly but with the realization that some may not. Don't forget that some students are not accustomed to following procedures and will test the waters until they determine that you, their teacher, are for real.

For this and any procedure to become a routine, the teacher must be consistent in insisting that it be implemented properly. This begins the next time the students enter the classroom. First of all, it is imperative that the teacher stand at the doorway greeting the students (see Procedure 4 in Part I).

Allow students to walk in—all of them—as you remain at the doorway greeting and welcoming them. It is important that you allow this process to unfold without interference even if some are not following the procedure. (That's right—no fussing!) Allow the bell to ring, close the door, and walk calmly to the front of the room. Instead of pointing out the deficiencies, begin by complimenting them for doing such a good job on their first "real" attempt. Let the actor in you emerge again! Do a cartwheel (if you can).

It's all right to tell them that there are still a few who did not quite implement the procedure correctly; then reassure them that you have confidence that they will improve with practice.

But what about in the future when they don't do it correctly? What does the teacher do then? Do not make the mistake of making them walk out and walk in again. If you do, you will have invited the students to engage you in a power struggle. Instead, talk to them privately and remind them about the procedure. Then tell them that if they "accidentally" forget the procedure again tomorrow, you will give up some of your recess time to practice it with them. (Do you see how nonthreatening this is? You also will notice that it takes only one time practicing with the teacher one on one for them suddenly to develop the skill of walking into the classroom appropriately.)

# Procedure 2
# for Teachers and Their Students:
# Tracking Tardiness

### Late Again

*Hurry so I won't be late*
*I can't make others sit and wait*
*Out of bed, I hit the floor*
*Grab my clothes and close the door*
*Breakfast this day won't be had*
*No "good-bye"s (I feel so bad).*
*Race to school and up the stairs*
*Down the hall (I brush my hair)*
*There's my class, the door is closed*
*The bell just beat me (by a nose)*
*With one deep breath I walk on in*
*"Sorry students, I'm late again!"*

*Elizabeth Breaux*

Remember that we are models for our students. We cannot expect our students to be on time if we are not on time!

Most school systems and/or individual schools have a predetermined "tardy" policy for students. This is especially important in middle and high schools, where students switch classes throughout the day. Most bell schedules allow several minutes for this transition from class to class to occur. A strict tardy policy is designed to keep students moving from one class to another in a timely fashion.

If you want to know which teachers in a school actually enforce the tardy policy in their classrooms, stand out in the hallway as the tardy bell rings. Some classroom doors will close immediately as instruction commences. Other classroom doors will remain open, with students loitering in the vicinity. There's no hurry to get to these classes because there are no consequences for being late. This loitering in the hallways most often becomes a distraction to the classes where instruction has begun, thus causing animosity between teachers.

Most school districts have a tardy policy in place. In that case, teachers must use it. It should be a rare situation to find a district or individual that does not have a predetermined policy. For the purposes of this section, we will assume that this school district has a tardy policy that is as follows:

- First Offense:      Parental contact
- Second Offense:   Lunch detention
- Third Offense:     *Office referral: in-school suspension
- Fourth Offense:    *Office referral: in-school suspension
- Fifth Offense:     *Office referral: out-of school suspension
- Sixth Offense:     *Office referral: out-of-school suspension
- Seventh Offense:  *Office referral: expulsion

Review the tardy policy with your students. Some of them may not be aware that there is a policy. Some may have come from another school district. Whatever the case may be, make certain that all the students are familiar with the policy.

*These consequences are always preceded by an office referral. It should never be the responsibility of the teacher to suspend or expel a student; instead, the teacher should refer the student to the administrator who will render the consequence.

## How to Teach It

Before the first day of school prepare a poster-size tardy chart for each class you teach. The chart must be large enough for students to see it from their desks or it will not serve its purpose, which is to keep students constantly aware of the number of tardies they have accrued.

When students arrive, assign each one a number. Never write their names on the charts. This is private information that should be shared by the students only if they choose to do so.

Once you have assigned a number to each student, review with the students the school's tardy policy. Refer them to the chart, which is already on the wall. Tell them that if they are tardy to class, a check mark will be placed on the chart next to their numbers. Tell the class that you will never place the check mark on the charts until the end of the day. This is done so that students won't learn other students' numbers.

Tell them that this chart is for them. Make certain they know that you also record tardiness in your roll book. This will stop them from acting on the urge to erase marks from the chart.

The chart will look something like the one shown here.

| Student | First: Call Parent | Second: Lunch Detention | Third: Office Referral: In-school Suspension | Fourth: Office Referral: In-school Suspension | Fifth: Office Referral: Out-of-school Suspension | Sixth: Office Referral: Out-of-school Suspension | Seventh: Office Referral: Expulsion |
|---|---|---|---|---|---|---|---|
| 1 | ✓ | | | | | | |
| 2 | | | | | | | |
| 3 | | | | | | | |
| 4 | | | | | | | |
| 5 | | | | | | | |
| 6 | ✓ | ✓ | | | | | |
| 7 | | | | | | | |
| 8 | | | | | | | |
| 9 | | | | | | | |
| 10 | | | | | | | |
| 11 | | | | | | | |
| 12 | | | | | | | |
| 13 | ✓ | ✓ | ✓ | | | | |
| 14 | | | | | | | |
| 15 | | | | | | | |

## How to Practice It

Tell the students that this is "pretend" time. Tell them that they are to exit the room and reenter as they would on a typical day. Ask a couple of them to pretend to be tardy. (They won't mind at all!)

Now pretend that the bell has just rung. All are in class except for the two you asked to arrive late. Go directly to your roll book and pretend to record a tardy mark next to these students' names. (Remember that you already told them that you would not record on the chart in the presence of others but instead would wait until the end of the day.)

At this time tell the students that if they are late for class but have an excuse from another teacher, they should bring the excuse to you immediately upon entering the room. That way you will not assume that they are tardy.

## How to Implement It

Begin *consistent implementation* on the next class day. Don't deviate from this policy. Some students will try you out to see how serious you are. Don't let them down.

If a student arrives after the tardy bell has rung and has no excuse, record it as such. Remember that the first tardy requires that you call the parent. Do it—that day! Often this is all it takes. The students now believe that you are for real. They'll stop testing you because they know that you will pass the test—every time!

Never in all of my years of teaching has one of my students been expelled from school because of tardiness in my class. It never got to that point. When students realize that the policy will be enforced, they adhere to the policy!

# Procedure 3
# for Teachers and Their Students:
# Implementing Bellwork

## A Better Way

*The bell just rang, what will I do?*
*My students are not seated*
*I've told them once, I've told them twice*
*And thrice I have repeated.*
*Late again, come three or four*
*While five or six throw paper*
*Mary helps to hand out books*
*But how long will this take her?*
*Paul and Kevin sharpen pencils*
*Others tag along*
*"Quiet, please, let's settle down"*
*This mantra is my song.*
*Surely there's a better way*
*I simply have not found it*
*But when I do, the world will hear*
*From mountaintops I'll sound it!*

*Elizabeth Breaux*

What is bellwork? It is exactly what the word implies. It's what we do *immediately* upon the ringing of the bell. It changes from day to day, but the basic format and procedure must be consistent. In more practical terms, *it's a lifesaver.* It "forces" the class to settle so that instruction can begin without wasted time.

Even more important to note is *what bellwork is not.* It is not simply meaningless busy work. On the contrary, it must be work that students know will be an integral part of that day's lesson. It is not time-consuming. It should last only a few minutes. It should never be redundant. Students should not be doing the same thing day in and day out.

**Bellwork is**

- What students do immediately upon arriving in class.
- Only a few (three to five) minutes in duration.
- Timed. Using a timer is a great idea because students know that the work must be complete when the timer buzzes.
- Meaningful. Students must know that their bellwork will be needed later on in the lesson.
- Easily accessible and understood. You should have a designated place in your room where the bellwork assignment is always written. This allows students to sit and begin working immediately each day.
- Worth something. Points should be awarded for bellwork.

## How to Teach It

Begin by talking to your students about bellwork. (Some of them will be familiar with the term, but some will not.) Have your bellwork chart or area already set up so that you can refer students to it during the explanation. They need to "see it." Impress upon them that the bellwork assignment will be written in this designated area daily and will be changed from day to day. (It is also important to have a bellwork assignment already posted. It will be used in the "How to Practice It" section, but you can refer to it in this section.)

Now go through the daily bellwork procedure with the students:

- Students should enter the room quietly, prepare their notebooks, and begin.
- Tell them that upon the ringing of the bell, the timer will be set for the designated amount of time and work must cease when that time has ended. (You will begin to notice that many will begin arriving ahead of time.)
- Tell them that you will place a red check (or another symbol) next to the bellwork daily. At the end of each week they will receive "bellwork points for the week," (You may choose to reward those who receive all possible points each week.)
- Tell them that the bellwork will be used as a part of the lesson each day.

*Note*: This is often where the breakdown occurs, so be careful. If the students don't view bellwork as being meaningful, they are more apt not to do it. I have observed many classes where bellwork was implemented ineffectively. Students viewed it more as meaningless "busy work" or a waste of time. Many simply were not doing it.

## How to Practice It

Remember that the bellwork assignment is already on the board. For the purposes of this practice section, let's assume that the bellwork assignment is as follows:

> *Turn to the story on page 12 of your text and read only the last paragraph. Think about what you know from this short passage. What are three things you would like to know? Write these three questions in your notebook.*

Begin by walking the students through a typical "beginning of class." (I would allow them to exit the room quietly and pretend that they are entering for the first time today.) Watch their every move. Guide them through this. Remind them to go directly to their desks, get out their notebooks, prepare their notebooks, read the bellwork assignment, and get busy. Remember to start the timer, placing it where all the students can see it clearly.

When the timer buzzes, have all the students stop immediately.

*Note:* Walk around during this short bellwork segment and place a red check above completed assignments. Then, once the timer buzzes, you will have only a few left to check. This not only saves time but lets the students know that you are watching and are interested in what they are doing. (Remember the teacher who sat at her desk while the students were working and then complained that the "students don't do their work"?)

In keeping with the definition of bellwork, use it in your lesson. The students were assigned a passage to read from a story that they now will begin reading in its entirety. Before that, however, have them share their bellwork "questions" with one another. This stimulates interest in the story that is about to be read. Instruct the students to look for answers to their questions while they are reading and to write the answers in their notebooks. This is true incorporation of the bellwork into the lesson. It has meaning, and students value it for that reason.

*Note:* Don't forget the "follow-up." Allow students to share their answers once the story has been read or during the reading of the story if it is being read in cooperative groups or with guided instruction from the teacher.

## How to Implement It

Begin implementation on the very next day. Since this may be new to many of your students, you may have to remind them as they enter the room, but most will remember. Don't deviate from proper implementation or they'll know it immediately.

You will notice that when the bell rings for the commencement of class, all is quiet. No direction will be needed from you because the students will know exactly what to do. All will be working, and life will be wonderful! You will be amazed at the attention-grabbing bellwork assignments you soon will be devising. Remember that it must be something that grabs their attention and is meaningful. Have fun with this. The possibilities are endless.

# Procedure 4
# for Teachers and Their Students:
# Taking the Roll

> *Rule 1 for calling the roll: Don't.*
> *Rule 2 for calling the roll: Don't.*
> *Rule 3 for calling the roll: Don't.*
> **Get the picture?**

Don't call the roll! Of course, we need some method for determining who is and who is not in our classes from day to day, but that old method of calling out names is an invitation for trouble, and who needs trouble at the onset of the class period?

Think about the many things that can happen during roll call, when the teacher must go through a roster of twenty-five or more names one by one. Do any of these sound familiar?

- Adam Adams is always first, right? (Poor child.) What does Adam do while the rest of the names are being called? Does he sit quietly? Probably not.

- Have you ever called the name of someone who is absent, and several students want to tell you where he is and why? (All different stories, of course.)

- What about calling the name of a student who is not absent but simply has not reported to class? Everyone seems to know where he "might be" and what he "might be doing."

- What about the class clown? You know the one. You call his name, and he screams out, *"present and accounted for!"* Everyone laughs, of course, even though he does this every single day.

- What about the student who tries daily to engage you in a power struggle by refusing to answer? What really bothers me about this scenario is that there are teachers who actually engage in the power struggle daily! They see the child sitting there, and so she is obviously "present!" So why the fight to the finish? Does the teacher need to "win" that badly?

The point is that we must find a way of taking the roll that does not involve calling the roll. it's that simple. Following are a few ideas:

- Create a seating chart. This is an "at a glance" way of taking the roll. An empty desk symbolizes an absent student. (This takes about ten seconds and can be done while students are working.)

- Check students at the door as they enter the classroom. (This can cause confusion, especially if you have very large classes. I've seen it practiced to perfection by a few teachers, but I've also seen it cause problems for others. Use caution if you decide to try this method.)

- Use class materials. For example, if your students write in their journals at the beginning of each class period, spread the journals out on the counter or table in advance. Instruct the students to pick up their own journals immediately as they enter the class, before sitting. Any journals (or whatever other materials you may use at the beginning of your class) left on the counter or table belong to students who are absent. You can record absentees in the roll book while students are journaling. No time is wasted.

- Use time cards. I used this method, and I and my students loved it. (Since it's my favorite one, I'll use it in the "How to" part of this procedure.)

## How to Teach It

Time cards must be prepared in advance so that they can be handed to the students on the day you teach this procedure. Once all the students have arrived and are seated, hand out the time cards.

Time cards should include the dates for one grading period (six weeks, nine weeks, semester, etc.). A time card serves a dual purpose in that it allows you to track both absences and tardies in a very efficient manner.

Another fringe benefit of time cards is that they serve as a constant reminder to students. Since the students literally pick up the cards each day, they are always aware of the number of times they have been absent and/or tardy.

Now that you have given each student his or her time card for the first time, explain to the students how the cards will be used. Let them know that you are the only one who will ever write anything on the cards. Explain the daily procedure:

- As they enter the class each day, they should pick up their time cards. (You may choose to spread them out on a counter for easy access, or you may want to set them on a wall rack the way it is done in the "real world," where employees actually have to punch in on a time clock.)
- Students should then take their time cards to their desks and lay them on the top right-hand corner of the desk.
- The teacher, of course, will wait until all are seated and the bell has rung and then will collect all the time cards that were not retrieved by students. An absence should be recorded on the cards immediately. If a student comes in late, the "absence" can be changed to a "tardy."
- After all recordings have been made, the teacher will pick up all the time cards from students' desks and return them to their holding place for the next day.

*Note:* Always use pencil when recording on the time cards.

An individual time card might look something like the one shown here.

| Name | Date | Absent | Tardy | Comments |
|------|------|--------|-------|----------|
| Adam Adams | 9/1 | | | |
| | 9/2 | ✓ | | Brought excuse from doctor |
| | 9/3 | | | |
| | 9/4 | | | |
| | 9/5 | | | |
| | 9/8 | | ✓ | Unexcused |
| | 9/9 | | | |
| | 9/10 | | | |
| | 9/11 | | | |
| | 9/12 | | | |
| | 9/15 | | ✓ | Excused—brought note from teacher |
| | 9/16 | | | |
| | 9/17 | | | |
| | 9/18 | ✓ | | Unexcused |
| | 9/19 | | | |

## How to Practice It

Now that all the time cards have been returned to their holding place, it's time to practice. (You may want to have the students exit the room and reenter, or you may want to call them by rows or groups to retrieve their cards.) Remind them to take the cards to their desks and place them on the top right-hand corner of the desk.

Then explain to them that you are going to pick up the cards that belong to students who are absent or tardy and record them in the roll book. After this you will retrieve all the cards from their desks and return them to their holding place. (Go through the entire process as the students watch.)

*Note:* Remember that your part in this (picking up the cards of absentees and recording them) can be done at your convenience. It should never take away from precious instructional time. This should be done only when students are working independently, allowing you to take a few seconds to complete this daily task.

## How to Implement It

As students enter your classroom the next day, remind them to pick up their time cards and place them on the top right-hand corners of their desks. That's it! That's really all the students need to do. The rest is up to you. You are going to love this procedure because it's so efficient.

There's one more perk that I forgot to mention. If you ever need to refer a student to the office for excessive tardiness (see Procedure 2 in Part II), there will be no questions asked. The student already knew that he or she was in trouble as a result of tardiness because the time cards have been a daily reminder. What actually ends up happening is that the students are so aware of their impending fate that they stop being tardy!

*Note:* In Procedure 2 in Part II, "Tracking Tardiness," you were given the chart method for tracking student tardiness, which probably would be used only if the time cards were not used. Both methods can be used, however, especially if you teach in a school where students are habitually late for class.

# Procedure 5
## for Teachers and Their Students:
# Sharpening Pencils

> ### Sharpening Pencils, Oh, What Fun
>
> *Sharpening pencils, oh, what fun*
> *This task requires more than one*
> *So off to sharpen, here we go*
> *(I always keep a friend in tow)*
> *And on the way we pick up more*
> *Friends, that is, just hear us roar*
> *Once we're there, the fun begins*
> *We get to meet a few more friends*
> *So if you're bored, do not despair*
> *The pencil sharpener's always there!*
>
> *Elizabeth Breaux*

Some of the best conversations in the world have taken place at the pencil sharpener. Some of the worst arguments have begun at the pencil sharpener. Have you ever noticed that pencil breaking is contagious? When one pencil breaks, others follow suit. What about all the lost instructional time?

For years I struggled to find a procedure that would alleviate the problems that often accompany pencil sharpening. I found several that worked, but never to my complete satisfaction, until the day my sister invented an ingenious procedure of her own. The search was over. Mission accomplished! Here it is.

## How to Teach It

In preparation for this teaching phase of the procedure, sharpen about twenty brand-new pencils and place them in a container. Place the container where it is easily accessible to you.

Tell the students that never again will they have to sharpen pencils. Tell them that they will be far too busy, and so you have decided to assume this task for them. From now on, whenever they need to have a pencil sharpened, they should give you the "I need my pencil sharpened" signal (thumbs up, raise pencil in air, or whatever works best for you). You then will grab a sharpened pencil from the container and swap pencils with them. Tell them that when you have time, you will sharpen their pencils for them. You will then return theirs to them, and they will give yours back to you. You then should return your nice new pencil to the container. That's it! No student will ever use the pencil sharpener again.

Remember that you don't need to be in a hurry to sharpen a student's pencil because the student has been given a sharpened pencil to use until his or hers is returned.

*Note:* You may want to invest in an electric pencil sharpener if you don't already own one.

## How to Practice It

Ask a couple of students to break their pencil points. They'll do it. No problem. No teacher has *ever* asked this of them before. In fact, the other students will be begging you to allow them to break their pencil points.

Ask all the students to pretend to work on an assignment. This is not a problem for them either. Many are masters at pretending to work! Now ask the designated "pencil-point breakers" to give you the "I need my pencil sharpened" signal. When they do, simply follow the procedure. Swap pencils with them, sharpen their pencils, and swap back. It's that simple.

## How to Implement It

Begin the implementation phase of this procedure immediately. The students have no problem catching on to this one. They love it because they think you are doing them a favor!

The only problem I have encountered with the implementation of this procedure occurs when the teacher forgets to sharpen his or her own pencils for the day. Don't forget to do this. It should become part of your morning routine. Just think of each pencil you sharpen as one less headache. Happy sharpening!

# Procedure 6
## for Teachers and Their Students:
# Using Classroom Materials and Supplies

### In Trouble Again

*I'm away from my desk to borrow a pencil*

*"Oops, I hit my friend"*

*Now, it seems, he's not too happy*

*And I'm in trouble again.*

*He hits me back, a fight ensues*

*My teacher runs to stop us*

*She grabs our shirts, we're hanging there*

*(I hope she doesn't drop us!)*

*She calls my mom, (who calls my dad)*

*Now I'm in hot water*

*From now on I promise that*

*I'll do just what I "oughter."*

*Elizabeth Breaux*

Keep all unnecessary movement around the room to a bare minimum. If you don't, you're asking for trouble.

After I had struggled for years to find a procedure to alleviate this headache, the light finally came on in my head! I decided to create "supply boxes" for my students.

I went to the dollar store and bought twenty-five of those small (approximately 8-by- 10-inch) plastic boxes. (You know the ones. They can be thrown across the room, used for punting practice, or beaten with a bat. They're unbreakable!) I filled each box with every item I could foresee using in my classroom (pen, pencil, scissors, glue, ruler, eraser, crayons, compass, protractor, highlighter, calculator, etc.) and placed one in each desk. I glued several name tags to the bottom of each box and wrote the desk number on each box to ensure that it remained in its proper desk. This procedure was in place on the very important first day when the students first entered my room.

You're probably thinking that this must have been a huge expense. Actually, it wasn't that bad. Several of the supplies were ones that I was given at school (calculators, rulers, pencils), and the others were extremely inexpensive (in the couple of weeks just before school starts especially). I, however, justified the expense I incurred by repeatedly telling myself that I would have spent a hundred times that amount in the therapy I would have needed if I had not come up with this idea.

Furthermore, I used this procedure for many years but never spent another cent of my own money. Here's how I managed that one.

## How to Teach It

When students arrive, familiarize them with the supply boxes. Have them remove the boxes from their desks, open them, and familiarize themselves with the items. Tell them that these boxes are for them. (If you teach more than one class, tell them that each box is also for any other student who sits in that desk later in the day.) All students love this, even the older ones. It's as though they've been given a gift. (What they don't know is that this is a gift that you have just given yourself!) Tell them that they are responsible for checking the box daily and telling you immediately if anything is missing. This, of course, means that the student in the last class "accidentally" left with something that belongs in the box. The teacher then can retrieve the missing item.

First, have them write their names underneath the boxes, where you have affixed the name tags. Then give them their supply lists, which include all the supplies and materials they are responsible for bringing in for the year. The list should include all or most of the items already in the boxes. As students bring in their supplies, the teacher can collect and stockpile the items in drawers or bins as replacements for the remainder of the year.

Once this is in place, replacement supplies are always readily available if a pen runs out of ink, a pencil becomes unusable, or a highlighter loses its "light."

Invariably, you will end up with many of the supplies left over at the end of the year. These, of course, are used to resupply the supply boxes for the next year. You get to keep your hard-earned money. Imagine that!

## How to Practice It

Have the students close the boxes and place them back in their desks. Tell them to pretend they have just entered the room. Remind them to sit, pull out their supply boxes, and check to make certain that all the supplies are there. Remind them that they should tell you immediately if something is missing so that you can retrieve it from the last student who used it.

Allow the students to use whatever supplies they will need for the remainder of this class period or day. At the end of the period or day instruct them to return all materials to the boxes. At this point the teacher should go through the list of all supply box materials so that students can make certain that all are there. (After a few days this no longer will be necessary because the students will have made a mental list themselves.) Tell the students to return the boxes to their desks before leaving the classroom.

## How to Implement It

When the students enter the classroom the next class day, remind them about the supply boxes. Remind them to check the boxes. Remind them to place everything back in the boxes and to place the boxes in their desks before they leave. Remind them, remind them, remind them. Soon they will remind you that you no longer need to remind them!

# Procedure 7
# for Teachers and Their Students:
# Distributing and Collecting Class Materials

### Wasting Time

*I can't decide where it should stay*
*These things that I must put away*
*On the shelves just yesterday*
*Yet in the drawers I placed today.*
*These for one class, those for the other*
*A final stack is for another*
*I can't remember which is which*
*From day to day they seem to switch!*
*The students try to help me out*
*"Wait, wrong class!" (I hate to shout)*
*"Hurry, please, we're wasting time!"*
*(I've lost my students and my mind!)*

*Elizabeth Breaux*

Stop wasting time distributing class materials. It doesn't have to be this way. With a little planning and organization the students can take over this job for you.

How often have you tried to place your hands on something that was no longer where you thought you'd placed it? Sound familiar? Have you ever wasted class time trying to get the proper materials in the hands of the students so that class could begin?

Waste time no more. Help is on the way, and it's sitting right in front of you!

## How to Teach It

*Note:* Before you can begin this teaching phase, you must have done the preliminary work: the planning, preparing, and organizing. Once that work has been completed, the students can take over the rest, with a little direction from you, that is.

On one of the first days of school, when you're ready to teach this procedure, ask for all the students seated at the back end of each row to stand. (If the students are seated in groups, you want to choose one from each group.) Ask these students to follow you as you show them around the room. (The other students should be asked to listen carefully, as they may be called upon from time to time to take over this responsibility.)

Literally explain where everything "lives" in the room. Your classes (if you teach more than one) should be color-coded; that is, each class should be given a designated color of its own. Whether you use shelving, cabinets, cubbyholes, bins, or any other storage device, the bottom line is that these "helpers" must know where everything is stored.

Now tell the students that when a particular item is needed, it will be their responsibility to distribute it to the students in their own row. For example, all students need their portfolio folders. The last student in each row rises, obtains the folders for his or her row, and makes certain that each student in the row receives his or her folder.

(There's a trick to picking up folders that makes it very easy for a helper to find the ones that belong to only those in his or her row. More on this in the "How to Practice It" section.)

Now that you are totally confused, let's try it. It works much better in practice than it does on paper, I assure you!

## How to Practice It

Let's do it now, using the portfolio folders as examples again.

Tell the helpers to please go to the back shelf or wherever you store your class items to retrieve enough folders for each one's individual row. (Remember that the folders are generic in nature, since there are no names on them yet.)

Tell the helpers to give one to each student on his or her row. Now have the students write their names on their folders. Explain to the students that these folders will be used throughout the year as portfolios in which examples of their writing will be placed.

It's time to return the folders to the storage area:

- Start by telling the students to pass the folders to the back of the row.

- Now tell the helper at the end of each row to stack the folders from his or her row on his or her desktop.

- Then tell the helpers to pass their stacks of folders to the right, remembering to keep their own stack on the top as others are passed to them. Once this process has been completed, the one helper on the far end of the room is holding all the folders in one large stack, with his or her row's stack on top.

- This last helper is the one who will place the folders back in the proper storage area.

*Note:* If this is done in reverse order the next time the folders are handed out, it will run like clockwork. Trust me on this, please. It works every time!

## How to Implement It

Use this procedure when distributing any of your class materials. The key is to have a predetermined storage space for all materials. Students must know where all items belong. Your job is simply to give the command. The students will do the rest for you. Never again will you will waste time looking for and handing out materials.

*Note:* Many teachers still feel the need to designate one student as the class helper. By doing this, you are placing a burden on one child to deliver materials in a timely fashion. The process invariably takes too long, and precious class time is wasted. It's much more efficient to have one student from each row do the job.

# Procedure 8
## for Teachers and Their Students:
# Getting the Students' Attention

Without the students' attention, we cannot practice our profession.

The bottom line is this: It doesn't matter how many years of experience you have accrued, how many degrees you have, or how much you know. If you cannot get the students' attention, all of it is worthless!

If we made a list of the ways in which teachers typically attempt to get students' attention, it would look something like this:

- ◆ Teacher asks students to stop talking.
- ◆ Teacher raises voice and asks students again to stop talking.
- ◆ Teacher speaks even louder in an attempt to be heard over all the talking.
- ◆ Teacher gets into a power struggle with students.
- ◆ Teacher begs and pleads with students to stop talking.

Any of these sound familiar? Often the problem is that there is no specific attention-getting procedure in place.

Several years ago I came across one of the best procedures for this that I have ever seen. I used it, and it worked—every single time! I will add, however, that the procedure continued to work because I insisted on the correct implementation every single day, no matter what. My students knew that, and they followed the procedure.

I came across this while reading Dr. Harry Wong's *The First Days of School*. It's called the "Give Me Five" technique. [1] In *The First Days of School*, it is explained as a five-step procedure in which the teacher stands in front of the students and raises his or her hand. The students then are required to do the following five things:

Eyes on speaker      Hands free

Quiet      Be still

**Listen**

For me, however, raising the hand was enough. The students knew exactly what it meant. If you had asked any of my students, they would have said that my raised hand meant "Stop talking and listen!" It worked for me. Here's how I did it.

## How to Teach It

On the first day of school, once all the students are seated, step to the front of the room, give them a big smile (don't forget this part), and hold your hand up in the air. Then do the following:

- Ask someone to tell you what it is that he or she just observed you doing. Invariably the student will say, "You smiled and you raised your hand." (Students often notice the smile first, by the way.)

- Then tell them that this is the signal for absolute quiet. If they ever see you with your hand up, whether in the classroom, in the hallway, in an assembly, or anywhere else, they should raise their own hands, cease talking, and give you their undivided attention. (Tell them that as soon as you see that all hands are raised, you will know that everyone is ready to listen.)

Go over this again. Tell them that no matter what they are doing, they should simply *stop, raise their hands, and listen.*

Now try it with them. They love this.

---

1  Harry K. Wong and Rosemary Tripi (1991). *The First Days of School* (p. 186). Sunnyvale, CA: Harry K. Wong Publications.

## How to Practice It

Tell them to talk! Yes, that's right. Tell your students that you need to have all of them talk. (They are definitely not accustomed to having a teacher request that they talk!) Really, encourage them. Walk around until you've got every single one of them talking. (What's funny is that when you ask them to talk, they suddenly get quiet.)

Now walk to the front of the room, smile, and raise your hand. The students will stop talking and raise their hands. They will do it. They always do. Praise them! Thank them! Practice it again. They love this, and it truly works.

## How to Implement It

You can now implement this procedure anytime and anywhere. I have seen teachers use it in their classrooms, in the lunch room, in the hallway, and even on the playground after the bell rings to reenter the building. It's great for assemblies, when the administrator needs the attention of hundreds of students at one time. It can become the universal procedure for an entire school or an entire school system.

I do a lot of speaking engagements, especially to large groups (several faculties at once). Whenever I know that I will be speaking and/or presenting for long periods that require breaks, I teach my audience this procedure. Then I use it to gather everyone back together. It works beautifully. If it works with several hundred adults, it'll work with anyone.

# Procedure 9
# for Teachers and Their Students:
# Getting the Teacher's Attention

> The students will attempt to get your attention by using any allowable means. Don't allow what's not acceptable.

Ask teachers to tell you the procedure that they want their students to use when getting the teacher's attention, and most will tell you that the students "must raise their hands and wait to be called on." I've never had a teacher tell me that he or she uses any of the following procedures:

- Students should scream at the teacher from across the room.
- Students should beat on the wall continuously until the teacher addresses them.
- Students should snap their fingers at the teacher.
- Students should interrupt a conversation between the teacher and another student.
- Students should simply tell others to shut up.
- Students should try answering more loudly than other students so that the teacher can hear them above the others.

Okay, you're laughing. I am too. We're laughing because many of us have allowed some of these ridiculous, hilarious "procedures" to occur in our classrooms. We all want students to raise their hands, but the students won't do that unless we insist on it. The only way to "insist" on it is to stop anything that is not acceptable—immediately! If you allow unacceptable behavior to occur even once, the students will realize that the teacher does not insist on implementation and that they have the option of implementing their own procedure. Don't let that happen. This is truly in your control. Don't lose that control by allowing what's not acceptable.

## How to Teach It

I begin the first day of school by telling my students that I have a problem of which I would like to make them aware. Once I say that, I have their undivided attention. They love it when we have "problems" because it makes us seem more real to them. I proceed to tell them that I have a hearing problem. I then tell them that this hearing problem occurs only when students don't raise their hands. (I give them a moment to process this, and invariably they smile when they realize what I am trying to say to them.)

After we all laugh a little, I tell them that I will always want their input in discussions but that I cannot hear them unless they first raise their hands and wait to be called on. Students understand this immediately. It's nothing new. They soon will know whether I'm for real or not. This depends on whether I follow through with the proper implementation of this procedure.

## How to Practice It

I begin by simply beginning class. I have a plan, however, and it works every time. Once a couple of minutes have passed, I throw out a question, perhaps something like this:

"What day is this again?" Invariably, several students will shout out the answer. I'll point to my ear and raise my hand, a simple gesture to let them know that I could not hear them. They understand my gestures, and they immediately raise their hands. I laugh with them and thank them for following the procedure. I also make certain to tell them, "It's okay to mess up on the first day. We'll all get it once we've practiced it a few times."

I continue with class and then pop a question like the previous one every now and then throughout the class period. After a few of these practice sessions they know that this is the procedure that will be followed throughout the year. They realize that I am for real: I say what I mean and mean what I say, and I do it all in a nonthreatening, congenial manner. I'm happy, they're happy, and life is terrific!

## How to Implement It

It's important to note here that some students may not be completely convinced. Continuous proper implementation, however, will convince even the greatest little skeptics. Just don't allow improper implementation. "Stop it in its tracks." "Ward it off at its inception." "Kick it to the curb." "Put a plug in it." And have fun while you're doing this. Tell the students that you'll remind them until everyone gets it right.

I assure you that this is an easy one. It normally takes only a day or two to have everyone on the same page. The students realize that the procedure must be followed, and they do it. "No questions asked!" (Pardon the pun.)

# Procedure 10
# for Teachers and Their Students:
# Encouraging Participation

## Mistakes Are Great

*Mistakes are great—we just can't wait*
*Till someone makes another*
*Each time they do, they help us to*
*Learn more and discover.*
*So let us take this mistake*
*And learn a lesson from it*
*For when we do, we're able to*
*Get up each time we plummet*

*Annette Breaux*

From *Real Teachers, Real Challenges, Real Solutions*

Let's be honest: No one likes to make mistakes. First of all, it's a blow to the ego. Furthermore, it's embarrassing, especially in front of our peers. The problem with making mistakes is that in society mistakes are unacceptable. How many times have you been commended for the mistakes you've made? If you had been, those comments would have sounded something like this:

- ◆ "Great job of being late for work, Ms. Breaux! Would you do that more often?"

- ◆ "Oh, thank you, Ms. Breaux for running that red light and slamming into my new car! My husband thanks you too."

- ◆ "Great new look, Ms. Breaux: one black shoe and one blue shoe. I think I'll try that tomorrow." (I actually did this once. The students loved it. We laughed all day!)

- ◆ "Don't even worry about having left the store with merchandise that was not yet paid for. People do it all the time!"

Have I made my point yet? In real life we pay for our mistakes and, one hopes, learn from them. In the classroom, however, students need to know that without mistakes, learning is not possible. So we need to encourage mistakes! Yes, you read this correctly: Encourage mistakes and you'll encourage participation!

## How to Teach It and How to Practice It

*Note:* You'll realize as you read ahead that the "How to Teach It," and the "How to Practice It" sections should be done together. The reason for this is that you don't want students to know that you are "teaching" them how to participate! What you are actually going to do is trick them into participating. (Don't you just love teaching?)

I have found a way to encourage participation without asking for it. That's right. In fact, I actually discourage it initially (I think this is called "reverse psychology"). No kidding. Here's how it's done:

- Begin by asking the students a question. Ask them to raise their hands if they think they might know the answer. Tell them immediately that they don't have to say the answer out loud. You are just curious about which students think they know it. Give them some time to think about the answer. Commend them as more and more hands go up. (By giving them this option, you've removed the fear of being called on to answer.)

- Now ask them to keep their hands raised only if they would like to answer the question. (Some hands will go down, I assure you, but some will remain raised. That's all right. You are beginning to encourage participation by taking away the fear of failure.)

- When students answer correctly, commend them.

- If a student answers incorrectly, thank that student profusely for attempting to answer. Tell the students that you believe that they are on the right track and then do everything you can to guide them to the correct response. That way, they will feel successful. (It is almost always within your power to guide a student toward the correct answer. If you simply cannot get a correct response out of the students, thank them again for the attempt and encourage them to continue trying.)

*Note:* This is the correct time to talk to students about making mistakes. Tell them that they will learn only when mistakes are made, and so you always will applaud mistakes. Let them know that you welcome their mistakes. Actually encourage them to make the mistakes! If you do, you are encouraging participation.

- Now you can begin asking the students a question and having them write the answer in their notebooks. As they write their answers, walk around the room while reading their responses. Assist any students who are having trouble. Make a mental note of those who rarely participate but do have a correct response.

- This is the time to call on the student who rarely volunteers to participate but who you now know for certain has the correct response. Something like this would be appropriate: "Jana, I read your answer, and it was excellent. Would you mind sharing it with the class?" Jana now has no fear of giving an incorrect response because you have proclaimed to everyone that her response is excellent. What you have just managed to do is take away a bit of that fear Jana possesses. She will become more and more likely to volunteer to participate in the future.

It is imperative that you spend some time discussing your "fear" that someone at some time may "unintentionally" laugh at and embarrass a student who gives a wrong answer. This is one of the "things" that will happen in any classroom where the teacher has not made it perfectly clear that laughing at others is not acceptable behavior. I used to set my class up for this "lesson" in the following manner:

- I would ask one of my students in advance to be my "guinea pig." I would inform this student of the question I was going to ask him or her and then present the student with an incorrect response that he or she was to give. I would tell the student that when he or she gave that answer, I was going to insult his or her intelligence by asking one or more of the following questions:
  - "Where have you been for the last thirty minutes?"
  - "What kind of ridiculous answer is that?"
  - "Please don't raise your hand again if you are clueless."

- After this, when all jaws have dropped to the floor, ask the students to explain to you what they have just witnessed. Encourage a discussion. Allow the students to tell you what they were feeling when they saw you treating their classmate so poorly.

- Ask your guinea pig to explain to everyone how he or she felt while this was happening. Invariably, your guinea pig will tell you that it was very uncomfortable even though he or she knew that it was a "setup."

- Tell the students that you remember the time when classmates laughed at an incorrect response you gave in class one day. Tell them that because of that incident, you were never again comfortable with participating in class. Also tell them that you remember the student who treated you so poorly and that he or she is currently serving a life sentence without parole!

## How to Implement It

It is of the utmost importance that you continue to implement this procedure in this manner throughout the year. What will happen eventually is that all the students will lose the fear of being wrong. This is the fear that has in their pasts carried with it many repercussions, none of them positive.

Continue giving students the option by telling them to raise their hands only if they think they know the answer, and then only if they would like to recite the answer. Invariably, what will happen is that more of the students will begin volunteering.

Use all the tactics you have in your bag of tricks to lead students toward correct responses. Remember to look for correct responses in writing, whether in notebooks or on tests, and call on the students you know have written the correct answer. Remember that even a student who has achieved a poor score on a test has answered a few questions correctly. Make notes while you are grading tests and remember to call on those who have the correct answer. This makes them feel good and encourages future participation.

Always remember that your classroom should be a safe haven for students, both physically safe and emotionally safe. Make certain that your classroom fills that bill.

# Procedure 11
## for Teachers and Their Students:
# Getting Students to Complete Homework Assignments

### I Didn't Do My Homework

*I didn't do my homework, and my teacher's really mad*

*Not about my homework, but the lousy excuse I had*

*It all started when I left my books inside my desk again*

*And instead of telling Mom the truth, I blamed it on my friend*

*I told her that my friend had brought my books home by mistake*

*But since I had no homework, no difference would it make.*

*So now my teacher asks for it, and again I tell a lie*

*One lie breeds another—there's no stopping it; I've tried!*

*"My mom was in the hospital, my dad was working late,*

*I had to watch the baby, so my homework had to wait."*

*She asks me if I realize that she wasn't born today*

*She saw my mom this morning, and so much she had to say.*

*She said my mom was feeling fine, my dad's been off for days*

*And my books are right there in my desk, where I left them yesterday!*

*Elizabeth Breaux*

From *Real Teachers, Real Challenges, Real Solutions*

Getting students to complete homework assignments consistently is a challenge teachers have faced since the dawn of time. It seems that regardless of where you teach or who you teach, you will have those in your classes who always do their homework, those who occasionally do their homework, and those who rarely do their homework. Finding a way to get students to do their homework consistently is a battle seldom won and often surrendered to the students. I can't tell you how many times I've heard teachers admit that they have given up. Problem solved: They have simply stopped giving home-work! Surrender no more, teachers: *Help is on the way.*

## How to Teach It

First, teachers, decide whether you want this done in individual groups or with the class as a whole. Either way works, but depending on the size and makeup of your class, one method may work better for you.

Create a large banner, using letters that can be removed and placed back onto the banner. In other words, don't write the letter on the banner with a marker but attach the letters to the banner. Place the banner on the wall on the day you plan to give your first homework assignment so that the students see it immediately upon entering the room. You may want to select one of the following phrases that I have seen teachers use:

Honorary Homework Heroes

Homework Rules

Homework Hotliners

Happy Homeworking

Let's assume that you choose to do this as a group. Tell the class that whenever a homework assignment is given, all the students are expected to complete it in the prescribed amount of time (usually by the next school day). Go to the banner and remove all the letters from it. Tell the students that they must earn back the letters by doing their homework. To earn a letter, all the students in the class (or in the group if you choose do this in groups) must turn in their assignments. If one student fails to turn in any assignment, the class (or the group) will not earn a letter that day. (Remember to make it clear that credit still is given on an individual basis.)

Here's the good part. Tell the students that they will win a pizza party, free library passes, free "go to the front of the line" passes, or *anything* that you know is worth winning (and that you can afford, of course) once all the letters have been earned back. You may want to allow the students to brain-storm some possible prizes or privileges that could be awarded.

## How to Practice It

Tell the students that you want to show them exactly how this will work and will need to have them to play along with you. Ask them to open their notebooks and say that you will pretend to check their homework. Have fun with this. Pretend to check each child's "homework." Compliment them all on their beautiful handwriting, correct answers, and so on. When you complete the procedure, pretend that all the homework assignments are complete. Then lead the applause! Go to the banner and add the first letter of your phrase. Remind them that once all the letters have been placed on the banner, the prize will be awarded.

*Stop!* You have not completed this practice session yet. It is extremely important to set some ground rules for students' behavior in case a student does not turn in the assignment, thereby stopping the entire class from receiving the letter that day. If this is not closely monitored by you, negative repercussions can occur.

Tell your students that instead of getting angry at a student who does not turn in the assignment, they should all work to encourage him or her to turn it in the next time. If you anticipate any problems from this, you may want to let the students know that if one student treats another poorly, a previously earned letter will be removed from the banner. This *always* works.

## How to Implement It

Give the first assignment. In my experience, once you practice this procedure with the students, they actually will ask you to give them an assignment. No kidding!

As the students enter your room the next morning, they will be asking you to hurry to check the homework. (Isn't that a nice turn of events?) Almost invariably, all the students will complete this first assignment. Don't miss this opportunity to compliment them, thank them, have them applaud themselves, and so forth. Remember that when we compliment students for doing a great job, they usually want to do it again.

Now place that first letter on the banner. Happy homeworking!

*Note:* In my opinion, homework should always be graded and not simply accepted because it was completed. Students must know that a certain percentage of the overall grade comes from the homework they submit.

# Procedure 12
# for Teachers and Their Students:
# Talking in Class (Use of Codes)

### What Does "Quiet" Really Mean?

*My teacher says to "quiet down,"*
*And many of us listen*
*But in no time we all begin*
*To talk without permission.*
*"I thought I said to quiet down,"*
*My teacher says again*
*("But we didn't know just what that meant,"*
*I whisper to my friend.)*
*What does "quiet" really mean?*
*What is "too much talking"?*
*When is it that it's not okay*
*To leave our desks for walking?*
*Sometimes you say there's too much noise*
*Sometimes we raise the roof*
*Sometimes you get so mad at us*
*And sometimes you're aloof.*
*We're not sure what we should expect*
*Could you be more specific?*
*And hurry, please, what we do next*
*May likely be horrific!*

*Elizabeth Breaux*

What does "quiet" really mean? No talking? Some talking allowed? Talking in a low tone of voice? Talking only until the teacher has had enough? If it means different things to different teachers, how are the students to know what's expected from class to class?

What can be even more confusing to a child is a teacher who has not decided what is allowed in his or her classroom! You know the teacher, the one who allows something to occur one day but becomes infuriated by the same behavior on another day. What about the teacher who allows the class to become completely unruly before attempting to put a stop to it?

While performing an observation in the classroom of a new teacher, I observed what I thought was one of the most clever noise-management strategies I've ever witnessed. Hanging from the ceiling in front of the classroom was an antique traffic light. (Upon inquiry I ascertained that the teacher had purchased it for a nominal amount from an antiques dealer.) I asked her to explain her use of that light, which I'll share in the "How to Teach It" segment.

*Note:* Not all of you will want to have a traffic light hanging in your classroom. Even if you did, what are the chances that you actually could find one? There are alternatives, however. Red, yellow, and green posters can be used in the same manner. Whatever you use as the signal, the rules of the game are the same.

## How to Teach It

Tell the students that "signals" will be used to specify allowable levels of talking in the classroom. Each signal has its own specific set of rules. The rules are as follows (post them for all to see):

Red signal: *STOP!* No talking allowed. Students may talk only to the teacher and must raise their hands (see Procedure 9 in Part II) to get the teacher's attention.

Yellow signal: *CAUTION!* Limited talking only. Students may be working in groups and may talk only to their own group members. They may raise their hands to speak to the teacher at any time.

Green signal: *GO!* Students are allowed to talk freely to others, but using low tones of voice. Movement around the classroom may be allowed, but with specified restrictions. Some activities require using the green light, but don't forget to practice exactly what is allowed when the green light is on.

Discuss each signal and exactly what is acceptable for it. You may add your own restrictions or rules to fit the needs of your class.

## How to Practice It

Tell the students that you now will practice using the different signals. This will give all of you the opportunity to iron out any potential problems.

Begin by placing the students in groups. Tell them that there are times when even though they are in groups, talking to one another is not an option. Explain that usually when they are in groups, they will be talking to other group members. Remind them that there will be times when it will be necessary to share what they are doing with other group members. All these situations require that a different signal be used. Now let's try it.

Give the students a group assignment in which they need to collaborate (possibly read and discuss a passage) as a group. *Turn on the yellow light!* Allow them to complete the assignment. Remind them that they may not converse with other groups when the yellow light is on.

Now *turn on the red light* and have them read the next passage silently. Remind them that they are not to talk once they have finished reading the passage, as others may still be reading.

Now *turn on the yellow light again*. Tell them to read the next passage together and formulate some questions of their own from the passages read so far. Tell them to answer and discuss the questions with their own group members.

Are you ready for this? *Turn on the green light!* Tell them that you want them to walk around and share their questions with other groups. If one group has asked a question that another has not, that question should be copied onto the latter group's page. Tell the students that you will give them five minutes to complete this task, at which time the red light will be turned on, signaling that all talking must cease and all students must return to their groups.

Once this practice session has ended, discuss it with your students. If you have any concerns, share them now. Tell the students that from now on, when they walk into the classroom, they should look for the signal.

## How to Implement It

As students enter your classroom the next day, remind them to check for the signal immediately. Don't make the mistake of expecting them to do that on the first implementation day or you will be setting them up for failure. Remember, they are not used to this, but if you gently remind them on the first day, they will comply.

As is likely to happen on most days (and should happen on most days), the red signal will be on as students enter the room. This will allow for bellwork to commence and/or for the teacher to share the objectives, activities, procedures, and so on, for the day.

Remember to *be consistent*. Insist that students adhere to the rules that are dictated by the signals. Don't deviate from those rules. If you do, your signals will become meaningless. It's up to you. Now turn on that green light and *"go."*

# Procedure 13
# for Teachers and Their Students:
# Managing Groupwork

> Groupwork: a group working together to achieve a common goal.

Imagine a house being built where all the carpenters built only walls.

Imagine an assembly line in an automobile factory where everyone installed only doors.

Imagine a school where all teachers taught the same subject.

My question to you is this: Why do we have students pull their desks together for groupwork and then give them all the same assignment? When we do this, we are defeating the purpose of groupwork.

In a true group activity all the students should be working toward a common goal or objective in a manner in which individuals go about achieving that goal or objective by using different means. In a true groupwork activity all the students contribute to a common goal but all are working on a separate "assignment" (while contributing to that common goal).

Let's take a group project, for example. If the groups consist of four students each, all should have their own group responsibility or task. The final "product" (the project) represents the efforts of all the students in the group.

Think about the implications of this. We are supposed to be addressing all the various learning styles in our daily lessons to reach all of our students, right? That's a difficult thing to do. We teach a total of twenty-five or more students at once. Some are kinesthetic learners, some are auditory learners, some are visual learners, and most are a combination of many different styles. Using the "true" groupwork concept, however, makes this possible. Each student's individual group assignment can be tailored to his or her individual learning style. Wow!

## How to Teach It

Teach this to the students by first placing them in groups. (It does no good to tell them about what they are "going to do." Instead, allow them to grasp it by placing them in the group situation while you are teaching it.)

First of all, you will need to have the first group activity completely organized with all group assignments, explanations, material, and so on, in place. It is also a good idea to have the classroom set up logistically when the students enter. Let's go through this step by step.

Imagine that all the preliminary work (the planning) has been completed. The bell has just rung, and the students are entering the classroom. Here's what you'll do:

- Tell them that there is a folder on each desk. Written on the folder are the names of all the group members. Each student should find his or her name and sit with that group.

- Once all the students are seated, tell them to notice that there is a number next to each group member's name. The member who is number 1 should open the folder.

- Notice that there are four separate assignment sheets in the folder, numbered 1 through 4. Group member 1 should give to each member the sheet whose number corresponds with that student's number.

- Tell the students to read the assignment that is on their particular sheets. Tell them to notice that there is a rubric/checklist (see Procedure 18 in Part II) that goes along with each assignment. At the bottom of the checklist they will find the number of points they can earn for their group by properly completing all the items on the rubric.

- Now tell them to share their "jobs" with other group members. It's important that everyone in the group know what the others are responsible for doing. Remember, this is a group effort. All the points earned by each member will constitute the group's final grade. This also forces group members to keep the others on task at all times.

*Note:* Think back to the old method of implementing groupwork in which the teacher simply gave the group an assignment and said, "Get to work." What usually happened was that one or two of the group members did all the work. This can't happen with the new procedure because all group members have separate jobs.

Make it clear to the students that each one is responsible for completing his or her own assignment, thereby contributing to the group. Once all the parts have been completed, you will assist them in putting the project together as a whole. Let them know that the overall grade will be the sum total of all group members' contributions.

## How to Practice It

Now you can have them place the assignments back in the folders and start from the beginning. Guide them again through the opening of the folder and the handing out of information. Tell them again to look at the assignment and the rubric/checklist. Allow them to practice adding the points of all group members together to figure the total possible points the group can earn. Also, prompt them to help one another by telling them to read the assignments of each group member and help one another decipher the rubrics. They should be encouraged to question you when that is necessary.

Let them begin the activity. Give them a lot of guidance. They'll need it this first time. Remember, you want this first group activity to be successful, so give them any help that will ensure that this happens.

## How to Implement It

I can say with the certainty that experience has provided that once you implement this groupwork procedure correctly, you will use it often. You will love it, and the students will love it. You will have little trouble getting students to participate in class activities.

You may even decide that this logistical makeup of your classroom will become the norm, creating a situation in which students work cooperatively in groups on a daily basis. The possibilities are endless. Have fun. Your students will!

# Procedure 14
## for Teachers and Their Students:
# Discarding Trash

## Garbage, Garbage Everywhere

*Garbage, garbage here and there*
*Garbage, garbage everywhere*
*Piled on the desks and heaped on the chairs*
*Filling the floor and creeping upstairs*
*Drowning my life and sucking my air*
*It's only a dream, but oh, what a scare!*

Elizabeth Breaux

## How to Teach It

It is imperative that students enter a clean and orderly room on the first day of school. This is when the precedent is set. What is even more important, however, is that they realize that it must be in the same condition when they leave it each day. Relaying that message lies solely in the hands of the teacher. Students can be messy. That's a fact. But another fact is that you, their teacher, are in complete control of what is and what is not allowed to occur in your classroom. Students will do whatever is allowed. Don't allow them to trash your room.

When teaching this procedure, call attention to the cleanliness and neatness of the classroom. Ask them to describe the room to you. Ask them to make assumptions about you that are based on the neatness and cleanliness of your classroom. Ask them to imagine your house and what it looks like. The students love doing this. (It also serves as a "get to know the teacher" activity.)

Allow the students to give descriptions of their bedrooms in their own homes. They really love this part. Have them draw pictures of their rooms at home and share them with one another. (Prepare yourself. This can be worse than a horror movie.)

◆ 105

Now tell them that you will grow horns and become a demon in the presence of garbage! (You're joking, of course, but they'll get the message.) Let them know also that you are there to serve them, and so you do not want them to have to walk to the garbage can at any time during the class period. Tell them that you want them simply to place any trash on the tops of their desks if there is room or on the floor right beside their desks. Tell them that while you are teaching and walking around the room, you will pick up any trash that has been generated.

Finally, let them know that when the bell is about to ring and they are about to be dismissed by rows, they should check their own personal space for trash, gather it, and throw it in the garbage can, which is *always* next to the door, as they leave the room.

## How to Practice It

Now that they've gotten the message, it's time to practice. Have a bag of trash (no food products or sharp items, please) handy for practicing this procedure. (They will love practicing this because they are already innately adept at creating trash!) Actually begin walking around the room throwing trash onto the floors and desks. (Yes, you can do this. You really can. It won't kill you. I promise. Just take a deep breath and do it!) Ask the students to place a piece of trash or two on their desks but to leave the rest scattered on the floor.

Allow class to begin as usual. While you are teaching, pick up some but not all of the trash while you are walking around teaching. When the bell is about to ring, remind the students that they are to gather any trash from their space and drop it in the garbage can as they leave the room. Watch them carefully as they do this on the first day and compliment them for being so helpful to you.

"But what about the power struggles that will certainly occur when no one wants to claim and pick up the trash in a particular space?" you ask. Here's my solution for that one.

Take the power away from them by telling them that if there is a dispute about "whose trash is for whom" and they cannot solve it in a mature fashion, they should alert you and you will come and pick up the trash yourself. This has worked every time for me, and it works in other situations also. (You know the situation in which one student passes a stack of papers to another, the papers fall, and they begin accusing each other, both refusing to pick it up? Same thing.) By showing them that this is not a big issue for you and that you don't mind doing it, you are taking all the fun out of it. Shame on you!

What eventually happens is that they pick it up themselves because they don't want to bother you with the task.

## How to Implement It

On the next class day remind the students of the procedure. Remind them that they will *never* need to leave their seats again to throw away trash. If you notice any students attempting to do this, just remind them. Remember that some of them are used to creating trash in some teachers' classrooms as an excuse to embark on a trip to the garbage can (a trip we all know can lead to just about anything). You have eliminated that forever! Good job. Now clean up your room before tomorrow!

# Procedure 15
## for Teachers and Their Students:
# Conducting Parent Conferences

In the typical "old school" style this procedure would be included in Part I, "Procedures for Teachers." Not so here. Read on to find out why.

Traditionally, parent-teacher conferences were strictly between the teacher and the parent. Even today this is the most appropriate method in some cases.

In this section, however, I would like to share a method of maintaining effective communication with parents that clearly involves the students in a manner that places much of the responsibility on them. It's called student-led conferences.

## How to Teach It

Prepare a "parent contact folder" for each of your students. Label the folders and prepare the inserts. Have all this in place before you give the folders to the students.

Distribute the folders. (Sit back and enjoy as you watch the students peruse the folders. They've never seen anything like this before, and the looks on their faces are priceless!) Allow a few moments for the shock to subside and explain to the students how these folders are to be used.

Begin by telling them that each folder will be an ongoing record of all conferences held with their parents. Tell them that they (the students) will be responsible for keeping the folders up to date. Now explain each of the inserts.

- Parent Contact Information Sheet:
  - Name of student
  - Name of parent(s)/guardian(s)

- Phone numbers (home, work, cell, etc.)
- Physical Address(es)
- E-mail address(es)
- Most appropriate call time(s)
- Most appropriate meeting time(s)

- ◆ Teacher Contact Information Sheet (to be brought home and given to the parents):
  - Teacher's name
  - Teacher's schedule (includes most appropriate meeting time)
  - School phone number
  - Home phone number (Some teachers prefer to have parents call them at home, but some do not. That's up to you. I always shared my home phone number and gave parents the option, but I made certain to stipulate that I did not take calls after nine at night. I never had a parent abuse this. In fact, I recall many instances in which parents thanked me for giving them the option, one that many of the working parents truly appreciated.)

- ◆ Conference Log: This is the part that shocks the students. Explain to them that they are responsible for leading the parent meetings (student-led conferences), helping the teacher predetermine the "points of discussion," and recording some of the pertinent information during the meeting. An example of a completed conference log is illustrated on the facing page. It will look something like this but can be tailored to meet your individual needs. (Notice that in the "Points of Discussion" column both positive and negative points have been included. Always include positives!)

Tell the students that you plan to meet with their parents throughout the year and that when you do, they (students) will be present and will lead the meetings. Tell them that they will help you determine in advance what the points of discussion will be. Tell them that they will lead the conference by explaining to their parents why the particular points of discussion were chosen. They will record under the "Student Agrees to" section and then pass the sheet on to their parents, who will record under the "Parent Agrees to" section and then pass the sheet on to the teacher, who will record under the "Teacher Agrees to" section.

It is vital to emphasize to the students that this conference is led by them; it is literally a student-led conference.

# Example of a Completed Conference Log

| Meeting Date | Points of Discussion | Student Agrees to | Parent Agrees to | Teacher Agrees to |
|---|---|---|---|---|
| 10/5/04 | 1. Tardiness | I will get up when my alarm goes off so that I don't miss the bus so often. | I will set my alarm and make certain that he is up on time. | I will call the parents to inform them of any further tardiness. |
| | 2. Enjoys reading | I will bring a book home every night and read before going to bed. I will keep a daily log of pages read. | I will allow him to join a book club and will take him to the public library weekly. | I will allow him to read a book whenever he is an earlier finisher on a given assignment and encourage him to share the book with others. |
| | 3. Good peer tutor | I will help anyone who needs help (without complaining). I will even help kids I don't like and will be nice to them. | I will allow him extra telephone time at night to be used strictly for assisting others who may need his help. | I will allow him to continue his peer tutoring and assist others in becoming peer tutors. |
| | 4. Lack of homework | I will write all my assignments down in a notepad and will show it to my mom every night. | I will check his assignment pad nightly and sign it. My signature will indicate that all homework has been completed. | I will check his assignment pad daily to make certain that all assignments for the next day have been recorded and to make certain that one of his parents has signed on the previous night. I will call home in the event of a missed homework assignment. |

Teacher's Signature:                Parent's Signature:

Student's Signature:

*Note: There should be several of these in the folder that can be used throughout the year.*

## How to Practice It

Let's try it. No parents are present, of course, so have the students pretend. They love practicing this one. Place them in groups of three or four. Groups of three, of course, would represent a student, a teacher, and one parent, and groups of four would mimic a meeting where two parents are present.

First, have each student fill out the first two columns on one of the conference logs: the "Meeting Date" column and the "Points of Discussion" column. Tell them to place at least two positives and two negatives in the "Points of Discussion" column.

*Note:* You can always find at least two positive things to discuss with parents about their children. Don't forget this part. It's vital! Unfortunately, many parents hear only negatives from teachers, and this causes a breakdown in communication. Parents want and need to hear what their children are doing right from time to time. Don't neglect to do this. They'll truly appreciate it, will be on your side from now on, and will be more than willing to help correct the negative behaviors.

Tell the students that they should take turns being the student, the teacher, and the parent. Allow them to practice. Once the rotation has been completed, all conference logs should be filled out. Allow them to share those logs with the class.

Tell the students that the next time they do this, it will be the real thing.

## How to Implement It

Begin implementation as soon as possible. I worked with a team of teachers who vowed to schedule a conference with each parent during the first month of school. This is not always possible, but it's a step in the right direction. If we can meet with parents soon and establish a good rapport from the beginning, the relationship is much more apt to be friendly, working, and caring.

As conferences with parents are scheduled, remind the students of the process. Remind them that they will be the leaders of the conferences. Work with them in advance to determine what the points of discussion will be.

Remember to explain this student-led conference process to the parents when you call to schedule a conference. They find it quite intriguing.

*Note:* From time to time you will be forced to deal with difficult parents. My suggestion is that you always ask an administrator in advance to sit in on a conference with any parent you feel may be difficult.

# Procedure 16
## for Teachers and Their Students:
## Calling Home

If students are allowed to use the school phone, they will come up with hundreds of reasons to do so. Remove the option and you solve the problem. Here's how.

This is a procedure that must be implemented schoolwide. Please share this with your administrator. He or she will thank you. The secretary will thank you. The parents will thank you. Other teachers will thank you. And the students will stop asking to use the phone. *Thank you!*

This has been in use for years in several of my district's schools that were lucky enough to hear about it. All the people who have used it can't believe that they didn't think of it themselves. It's so basic and so simple. You're going to want to claim it as your own.

### How to Teach It

On one of the first days with your students, give each of them a copy of the "Call Home Form." An example is shown on the next page.

Explain to them that this is the form they will have to fill out if they need to call home. Tell them that, for instance, if they are sick and need to call home, they should tell their teacher, who will give them one of these forms to fill out. Once it is filled out, they should return the form to the teacher.

Here's the really ingenious part: The teacher will give it to another student, who will carry it to the office. That student will give it to the secretary or clerk, who will make the call. Students never get to use the phone!

| | | | |
|---|---|---|---|
| Name of student | | Name of parent(s) | |
| Sending teacher | | | |
| Date | | Phone number(s): | home |
| Time | | | work |
| | | | cell |
| | | Email address | |
| | | | |

| | | | |
|---|---|---|---|
| | | **Student's Schedule** | |
| 1st Period: | | 4th Period: | |
| 2nd Period: | | 5th Period: | |
| 3rd Period: | | 6th Period: | |

Reason for calling home: _____

_____

_____

In case you haven't figured out why everyone is in love with this procedure, here's why:

- The *secretary* loves it because no longer are there lines of students coming to the office to use the phone. When she or he receives the form, a call home is made immediately. When and if the parent arrives to pick up the child, the secretary simply looks at the Call Home Form to see where the child is at that time and notifies the child that the parent is there to pick him or her up.

- The *teachers* love it because this method stops students who just want to take a walk from even asking to use the phone. It's no use because someone else will be taking the Call Home Form to the office!

- The *parents* love it because their children are not calling home all day long for frivolous things.

- The *administrators* love it because the students who were usually the ones out of class no longer have a reason to leave. The hallways and the office areas are much more orderly.

## How to Practice It

The only practice necessary for this procedure is the actual filling out of the form. Since the students are required to do this, allow them to fill out the form in its entirety. Walk them through it. Make certain that *all* the items are specified. (You do not want to have to use precious class time in the future to assist in the filling out of the form, but you always want to glance over it before sending it to the office with another student.)

## How to Implement It

You may want to suggest to your administrator that he or she send this form to the local printing facility to have it printed on glued notepads, which usually can be printed in booklets of any size. This way all the teachers can be given a pad that can remain on their desks within hand's reach.

Once the booklets have been printed and the administrator is ready to begin implementation, it's important to explain the procedure to all the staff members in one forum. As with all schoolwide procedures, it is vital that all teachers implement the procedure in the same manner.

After this initial meeting, begin the implementation immediately. Everyone will love you for it.

# Procedure 17
## for Teachers and Their Students:

# Requesting
# Water and Bathroom Privileges

> What goes in must come out. It stands to reason that if we allow students to leave the classroom to get a drink of water, we will have to allow them to leave again to get rid of that drink of water.

I am not asking you to be insensitive to the "needs" of your students, but I will say to you what I've said to my students for many years: "I have never seen a student die of thirst during a one- or two-hour class period." It just doesn't happen.

"Drink your water at recess if necessary, but *never ask* to miss precious class time to do so!" This is something that we must make clear to our students from the beginning. They will test you. If you begin allowing students to leave the room for water, it will become a procedure. That's right—the "procedure" for leaving your room will simply be to *ask for water*. (If a child is choking and needs water, please disregard the above.)

This leads to the second issue: requesting bathroom privileges. Again, use your discretion about what might be an emergency. This too must be communicated to the students from the very beginning. I always said this to my students at the start of the school year: "If you feel you are about to embarrass yourself in front of the class, please let me know. This is what we consider an emergency! Other than that, please don't ask."

I always ended this very brief discussion by saying to the students, "If you *ever* see me just get up and leave the classroom, please notify someone that there is an emergency." You see, I knew that I needed to model for them my belief that instruction is far too important to miss except in an emergency.

## How to Teach It

It's very important to communicate to the students your personal feelings about the value of instructional time. They must know that you will not allow anything other than an emergency situation to interfere with instruction.

While you are talking to them about this, let them know that you will never leave the classroom except if there is an emergency and that you expect the same from them. Let them know what you consider an emergency. Actually say the following to them:

- ◆ "An emergency situation is one that requires that you leave the classroom immediately. If you ever feel that you are about to embarrass yourself in front of others in the room, please ask to leave! If this is not the case, please respect the need for uninterrupted instruction."

- ◆ "Of course, going for a drink of water will be an emergency only if you are about to choke to death. If that is not the case, please refrain from ever asking to leave to get a drink of water."

*Note:* This procedure can be implemented only in a departmentalized situation in which students are switching classrooms every hour or so, thereby having the opportunity to go to the restroom during the "breaks." If you teach in a self-contained environment, you may need to schedule restroom breaks during the day. My suggestion is that you take the entire class to the restroom at once, thus avoiding the possibility of students abusing the privilege.

In case you were wondering, the procedure for going to the restroom during class time is simply this: "You don't, except in the case of emergencies, in which case you walk very quickly!"

## How to Implement It

For obvious reasons, the practice will be in the actual implementation (unless you want to practice emergency situations; my guess is that you don't).

You do want, however, to make certain that your students know that you will implement this procedure, and, as with all children, they will test the water (no pun intended) at first. When that first student asks to be excused to go get a drink of water, remind him or her that students should never ask to leave unless they are choking.

When that first student asks to go to the restroom during class, remind the students that they should leave only if it is a dire emergency.

If you follow this procedure by insisting on its proper implementation, you will set a precedent from the beginning. Students will know that the procedure is implemented at all times, and the waters they are testing will remain in the fountains.

*Note:* Make certain to adhere to the hall pass procedure that has been determined by your administration. Some schools use agenda books as hall passes. Some schools use an actual form. Whatever the case, always follow the schoolwide procedure.

# Procedure 18
# for Teachers and Their Students:
# Taking a Test

### The Test Is for the Teacher

*My teacher likes to teach me things*
*And test me when we're through*
*She says the tests are for her too*
*She uses them as proof.*
*Proof that she has taught me well*
*Or needs to teach me more*
*This, she says, she often can*
*Determine from my score.*
*For if my score is not so good*
*More work we need to do*
*She rolls her sleeves and pulls a chair*
*Her tactic now is new.*
*She's bound and she's determined*
*That we both will do our best*
*I assure her that "we" will do better*
*On tomorrow's test!*

*Elizabeth Breaux*

Is the test really for the teacher? Of course it is. (Just don't let the students know that!) How else would we know whether we're doing a good job? The proof of any job well done is in the product—and the children are our product!

Students, of course, must be made to realize that assessments are tools used to determine their proficiency levels. Without authentic assessment, that would be difficult to determine. On this account, testing is used to see what the students know or have learned.

If we simply were to teach, test, and then move on, we would risk leaving many students behind. It is imperative that we use our testing results for reteaching purposes, for reflecting on the strategies that we used, and for planning additional strategies that will address the various learning styles and ability levels.

*Question:* What exactly is a test?

- Is it that two-week summation of work all piled into one testing day?
- Is it a question or two at the end of any lesson?
- Is it a series of questions, both verbal and written, throughout the lesson?
- Can it come in the form of an activity?
- What about a project?
- Is it something we take before we begin the lesson?
- After we've completed the lesson?

*Answer:* All of the above. Tests or assessments come in all shapes and forms. On the days when we give a written test, however, we must have a procedure in place so that everything runs smoothly.

## How to Teach It

Students must be "taught" our test-taking procedures. Unfortunately, we often leave them in the dark, assuming that they already know. Instead, take some time to talk to them about this.

Tell them that on testing days all materials will be left in their book bags or desks. On these days you will make certain that they receive all the testing materials that are needed. Tell them that test-taking time is "quiet" time. Talking is not an option unless they are speaking to you. (Use the red code from Procedure 12 in Part II.)

Show them a sample test and guide them through it while leading a discussion on good test-taking strategies:

- Insert the heading on the test.
- Read the directions. Ask questions if necessary.
- Check for specification of points on individual test items.
- Study the grading rubric/checklist. Many students may not be accustomed to using one of these. Here is a sample of what a rubric for grading a paragraph might look like:

_____ The paragraph is indented. (1 point)

_____ A good topic sentence has been written. (1 point)

_____ Sentences 2, 3, and 4 are details that support the topic. (3 points)

_____ A good closing or wrapup sentence ends the paragraph. (1 point)

_____ Punctuation is properly used. (5 points)

_____ Capitalization is properly used. (5 points)

_____ All sentences are complete sentences. (5 points)

Possible Points: 21

Points Earned:_____

Your Score: _____

_Note:_ When students are given a rubric, expectations are clear. They know exactly what they are to do, and they do it every time! The greatest fringe benefit of using a rubric is that it makes the assessment easy to grade.

- Complete the test.
- Recheck the grading rubric to make certain that everything has been addressed.
- Raise your hand when you are ready for the teacher to collect your test (never allow students to leave their desks during testing time).
- Get to work while waiting for others to complete their tests (see Procedure 19 in Part II).

## How to Practice It

Using a multimedia or an overhead projector, show students a sample of one of your tests. Walk them through the entire process. (Refer to the list above.)

- Have one of the students read the directions and then have that student tell you exactly what is being required.
- Check test items or sections for specifications of points and discuss.
- Examine the rubric/checklist and discuss.
- Now literally complete the test with them.

_Note:_ I actually walked them through this process again on their first graded test! I guided them through the entire test, stopping to explain everything. I made certain to allow them to answer the questions individually and without assistance from others, but everything else was in the form of a detailed explanation. What this did was assure me and my students that everyone was following the procedure properly from day 1, test 1. Therefore, I didn't have to go back and "fix it" for those who got it wrong that first time.

- Once all the students have finished answering the test questions, guide them through the rubric/checklist, reminding them to go back and double-check to make certain that everything on the list has been completed.

- Remind the students to raise their hands upon completion of the test so that you can collect it.

- Remind them that they should get to work on their "early finishers' assignment."

## How to Implement It

This should be a breeze. You've already taught the procedure and practiced it in the real-life format (since you've already guided them through the first test).

It's their first time doing this alone, however, so discuss the procedure again before handing out the test. Make certain that they all understand exactly what is required. Encourage them to ask procedural questions if necessary. You want this to run smoothly for the remainder of the year. Set the stage now. Good luck on the tests!

# Procedure 19
## for Teachers and Their Students:
# Providing for Early Finishers

### What Should I Do?

*My work's complete, my day is through*
*But time remains, what should I do?*
*I'd watch the clock, but that's no fun*
*I'd read a book if I had one*
*My teacher says I cannot talk*
*She'll never let me take a walk*
*I'm running out of options here*
*What I'll do next is what I fear!*

*Elizabeth Breaux*

Nothing good can come from idle time. Some of the worst classroom disasters have occurred when students were not actively involved in something meaningful. Too often we forget to plan for early finishers. We give an assignment, and invariably the same students are the first to finish. We must have something meaningful planned for these students or their active little imaginations are likely to devise a plan of their own.

Don't confuse "idle" time with "free" time. Free time can be just that—a time when the students choose (with the choices given by the teacher, of course) an activity. You, the teacher, must plan those activities or choices in advance. Students must know that idle time is *not* an option.

## How to Teach It

Give an activity folder to each student and have him or her write his or her name on the front cover. Tell the students that these folders are to remain in the classroom at all times but are theirs to use for the remainder of the year. Talk to them about when and how these folders will be used.

Let them know that these folders are to be used only when the classroom assignments have been completed and checked by the teacher. Don't skip this part! Students must know that they will never be allowed to use their activity folders until you have checked to make certain that the classroom assignments have been completed. This will deter students from rushing through assignments.

Allow them to open the folder and peruse the activities. Be certain that you have placed a variety of enjoyable yet educational activities in the folders. Activities could include (but are certainly not limited to) the following:

- Journal writing where fun prompts are given
- Crossword puzzles
- Silent reading time (novel, magazines, etc.)
- Computer time where a website and an assignment are given
- Mathematical word problems
- Brain teaser activities

Now show the students where the activity folders will be housed in the room. Make certain to choose an area that is easily accessible to them. (You may want to consider distributing the folders at the beginning of each class period. This will eliminate the movement that would occur when students are retrieving the folders themselves.) Pick up the folders (see Procedure 7 in Part II).

*Note:* Don't forget that you will need to replenish the activities in the folders from time to time.

## How to Practice It

Give the students a short assignment to complete. Tell them that they must show the completed assignment to you before they begin using their activity folders. Allow them to begin. As students begin raising their hands (see Procedure 9 in Part II), quickly check to make certain the work has been completed. (This should be a very quick process since you are not grading the material at this time.) Allow the finishers to begin working in their activity folders.

Once all the students have completed the initial assignment, signal to them to put their activity folders aside, as class will resume. The folders should be collected at the end of the class period and placed in the predetermined location (see Procedure 7 in Part II).

## How to Implement It

Begin consistent implementation on the very next day. You will, as with all procedures, need to remind them of the process.

Begin to notice which students are habitually the earliest finishers and provide more activities for them. Activities eventually (once you get to know your students) should be tailored to the specific interests and needs of the students. Never let the activity folders become barren or boring. They should be filled with interesting activities that are not only educational but fun. Don't make the mistake of allowing these folders to become filled with "busy work." The students will view them that way, and you will have a new problem on your hands.

# Procedure 20
## for Teachers and Their Students:

# Taking Responsibility for Recording Grades

> Students typically remember the last grade, *whether* it was good or bad. If the last grade was an A, they think they have an A average.

Have you ever experienced the wrath of a student on report card day? You know, the student who is furious (with you, of course) about his or her poor grade. Want to stop this from ever happening again? Here's how.

Create grade sheets for students and place them in individual student folders. Create these folders in advance so that they are ready on the day that you want to begin teaching this procedure. A sample of a completed grade sheet is illustrated on the next page.

## How to Teach It

On the first day a graded assignment is completed and handed in by the students, give a grade sheet to each of them. At this time explain to the students that all recording of grades on these sheets will be done by them. Tell them that tomorrow, when you return the graded assignment to them, they will receive the sheets again. They then will be responsible for recording their own grades on the sheets. Remind them that you, of course, keep track of grades in your roll book. This immediately takes away the inclination some students have to record a grade improperly. There's no reason to do that because it won't matter. You use the roll book for averaging grades. This grade sheet is simply a tool to keep them apprised of their averages throughout the grading period.

Tell the students that each time a graded assignment is returned to them, grade sheets will be distributed. At that time they will fill in the "Date," the "Possible Points," the "Earned Points," and the "Letter Grade" sections.

| Name_____ Grading Period _____ | | | | |
|---|---|---|---|---|
| Subject_____ | | | | |
| Date | Description of Assessment | Possible Points | Earned Points | Letter Grade |
| 11/3 | Written Test on "Sounder" | 100 | 96 | A |
| 11/17 | Quiz on Story Elements | 20 | 18 | B |
| 11/21 | Group Project: Character Analysis | 50 | 40 | C |
| 12/2 | Novel Summary | 100 | 88 | B |
| 12/16 | Poetry Analysis | 10 | 9 | B |
| 1/6 | Essay Addressing A Prompt | 100 | 74 | D |
| | Total Possible Points | 380 | | |
| | Total Earned Points | | 320 | |
| | Final Average | 84% = B | | |

Take this time to teach students how to average grades. (Many of them, even the older ones, still don't understand how this is done. They still think that teachers "give" grades. I always told my students that they are the ones who give the grades to me. I simply record what they give me!) Show them how at any time during the grading period they can average their own grades by doing the following:

- Figure the total number of "possible points" to date.
- Figure the total number of "earned points" to date.
- Divide the "earned points" by the "possible points." That's your average.

The students can't believe it's this easy!

## How to Practice It

Return a graded assignment. At that time hand out the grade sheets. Walk the students through it as they fill in their own information. Pick up the grade sheets.

The next time you return a graded assignment and students record their grades on the grade sheets, remind them to do a quick check of their overall averages. (They will need your assistance, but let them actually do it.)

You may need to walk them through this procedure the first few times, but it won't be long until all of them are comfortable implementing this procedure on their own.

## How to Implement It

You will notice that students will begin taking full responsibility for their own grades and averages. For the first time they really see how grades are given.

They no longer blame you for poor grades. In fact, the greatest benefit this procedure provides for the students is an awareness that they never before possessed. By using the grade sheets, students are kept aware of their averages and know what needs to be done to improve those averages (if necessary).

The students will never again blame you for a poor grade. In fact, grades miraculously improve as a result of their heightened awareness!

# Procedure 21
## for Teachers and Their Students:
# Providing for Substitute Teachers

> "Students often 'substitute' their personalities for less desirable ones in the presence of a substitute teacher."
>
> From *Real Teachers, Real Challenges, Real Solutions*

## How to Teach It

Explain to the students that there will be times during the year when you may be absent from school. Talk to them about the importance of having the class run smoothly in your absence. Let them know that you have a plan and that the plan requires that they take responsibility for helping to ensure that the class runs smoothly in your absence.

Tell the students that they will be given roles and responsibilities they must carry out in your absence. Allow them to help with the makeup of this list. You may want to allow them to have input on the types of jobs, roles, and/or responsibilities that will be filled. This way they feel that they have a vested interest in the whole procedure.

Once you and your class have devised a list of job descriptions (see the sample list that follows "How to Implement It"), begin assigning jobs to students. Let them pick their own jobs as much as possible. You may want to pair students for certain jobs. If you teach more than one class during the school day, you will have to go through this process in each class. It is important that lists be posted on the wall once they have been devised.

"Sell the process": Pump them up; have faith in them; show excitement about the process.

## How to Practice It

The students absolutely love to practice this one. (The good news is that you can work it into your lesson plan by using the subject matter for that particular day.)

After the students are comfortable with their individual responsibilities, tell them that you will have a "practice day" in which they will pretend that you are the substitute. (You need to put on the actor's hat and pretend. It's imperative that you give them the power!) Remind them several times during the class period that tomorrow will be "Practice with the Sub Day."

When they arrive on the following day, begin pretending. (One teacher I know even wore a wig and a very uncharacteristic outfit that day so that the students would have no trouble pretending he was someone else.) Let them help run the class. Let them assist you as they would assist the substitute teacher. They can and will.

You will want to use the next class day as a follow-up. Take a few minutes to critique the previous day and iron out the kinks with the students. You will be pleasantly surprised at the suggestions they will have.

## How to Implement It

This procedure may require some polishing up throughout the school year. The best-case scenario provides that you know in advance that you will be absent. That's when there are usually no problems because you are able to tell the students the day before and use a few minutes of class time for a short practice session.

To be prepared for an unexpected absence, however, you need to make certain that you occasionally do a spot check with the students throughout the year. You want to make certain that they are always prepared.

It is equally important that you constantly keep your substitute materials up to date. If you keep up your end of the bargain and assist the students in keeping up their end of the bargain, chances are that you will never again have one of those "return to school after an absence" days when you return only to find that your little angels have become demons in the hands of the substitute teacher.

### Suggested Roles and Responsibilities

These are just suggestions. You should tailor this list to fit your needs.

- *Greeter:* This student welcomes the substitute teacher.

- *Hospitality assistant:* This student takes the sub on a tour of the classroom and points out where materials are located.

- *Sounder of silence:* This student explains and models the procedure (for the sub) for getting the students' attention.

- *Roll call attendant:* This student assists the sub in taking the roll.

- *Seating chart monitor:* This student helps the sub ensure that all the students are in their assigned seats by helping the sub check the seating chart.

- *Distributor:* This student assists the sub in handing out materials.

- *Practitioner:* This student explains any relevant class procedures to the sub (throwing away trash, pencil sharpening, exchange of classes, agenda book, tardy policy, etc).

- *Collector:* This student picks up all materials used during the hour, places them in the correct folder, cubby hole, or place, and reminds the students to discard all trash when leaving the room.

- *Cheerleader:* This student thanks the sub on behalf of the class and begins the round of applause.

- *Rewarder:* This student gives the sub a small token of the class's appreciation. (This should be left in a designated area where the child can access it easily. The gift may be a bag of popcorn, a candy bar, soda money, "freebies," etc.).

# Procedure 22
## for Teachers and Their Students:
## Attending Assemblies

### A "Sick Day," Anyone?

*I'm going to take a "sick day,"*
*And I'll do it sometime soon*
*I'm leaning toward the end of March*
*That's the next full moon!*
*If you've taught for any length of time*
*You know just what that means.*
*The moon might be our friend, sometimes*
*But not when he's full steam.*
*The full moon's wrath is vicious*
*A demon to our schools*
*He turns our angels inside out*
*Transforming them to ghouls.*
*The only thing that could be worse*
*(The results have been quite steady)*
*Is a schoolwide assembly!*
*I'm feeling sick already!*

*Elizabeth Breaux*

Procedure 22

It's safe to say that many teachers cringe at the thought of a schoolwide assembly. If you are one of those teachers who schedule your "sick days" around schoolwide assemblies, this procedure is for you!

*Note:* It is important to realize that this procedure must be practiced schoolwide. If you are teaching in a school that has not established an effective procedure for schoolwide assemblies, you may want to approach your administrator with this one or some variation of it tailored to suit your particular needs.

This will require some preliminary work on the part of the faculty before it can be taught to the students. Once a committee tailors the procedure to fit the needs of your school, it will have to be shared with the rest of the faculty.

These are some suggestions on how you can set up this procedure for your school:

- Divide the assembly area (gym, cafeteria, auditorium) into sections: one for each class.

- Assign each teacher or class to a section. (This is critical. Don't place "troublesome" classes near one another. Don't place grade levels together. Instead, place a first-grade class next to a third-grade class or a fifth-grade class next to a seventh-grade class.)

- Assign each teacher a "point of entry" to the assembly area. For example, if there are four points of entry to the gymnasium, have teachers come in from the door that is closest to their section, thus spreading out the confusion.

- Call classes to the assembly by section numbers. Make certain you are calling from different areas of the campus and from the various sections (in reference to seating). Therefore, there will be no "clogging of arteries" (both yours and the hallways and entryways). For instance, instead of calling for sections 1 through 5 to report to the assembly, call for sections 1, 6, 10, and 13. That way, when they enter the assembly, they are not all trying to get to the same general area.

Now that the faculty is on the same page with the procedure, it's time to teach it to the students.

## How to Teach It

Tell the students that you are going to discuss with them the procedure for attending an assembly. Then go through this list with them:

- Assign an "assembly" number to each student. (This is *not* the "section" number. This is the individual number that the students will use to form their lines for walking to the assembly. It will assist you in ensuring that certain students do not sit next to each other.)

- Tell them that on the day of the assembly they will line up in single file according to their numbers. They will sit in the same order once they arrive at the assembly.

- Now tell them that their class has been assigned a certain section where they will sit in the assembly. When the principal calls their section number, they will line up and report to the assembly.

◆ Talk to your students about proper behavior and etiquette when attending the various types of assemblies: guest speaker, pep rally, basketball game, music concert, and so on. Behavior and etiquette requirements will vary with the type of assembly the students are attending.

## How to Practice It

My suggestion is that you wait to practice this procedure until a day or two before the first assembly. That way the procedure will be fresh in their minds. It is also a good idea to practice it again before the next assembly and possibly even the one after that, especially if there will be more than a couple of months or so between assemblies.

When practicing, remind the students first of their assembly number. This is the number that determines the line order. Have them line up in that order. Walk them to the assembly area and allow them to sit in the proper section (if the assembly area is set up as it will be for the assembly). A good time to practice this might be just before going to recess or just before bus dismissal. That way you are not using precious class time for the follow-up practices.

*Note:* For most classes a simple reminder before each assembly will be enough practice.

## How to Implement It

Make certain to "remind" your administrator to "remind" the rest of the faculty to "remind" their students of the procedure shortly before each assembly! Everyone must be on the same page with this procedure if it is to work. The overall implementation is beautiful if everyone does his or her part.

Now cancel that "sick day" and enjoy the assembly!

# Procedure 23
## for Teachers and Their Students:
# Behaving in the Cafeteria

### The Lunch Room

*Apple sauce glued to my hair*
*Bubble gum stuck to my chair*
*Banana peels in flight in midair*
*This lunch room is in disrepair!*
*Milk and juice smeared on the floor*
*Yesterday's lunch to class I wore*
*My angels, rotten to the core*
*This chaos I can stand no more!*

*Elizabeth Breaux*

It has been my experience that most schools have a schoolwide procedure for behavior in the cafeteria, but as with any procedure, it's only as effective as the person implementing it.

What if there is no schoolwide procedure in place? Well, like all effective teachers, we devise one. We "invite" others to join us. The bottom line, unfortunately, is that we can only be models of excellence and hope that others will follow in our footsteps. Believe me, when others see how effectively this works, they'll beg you for your secret.

First of all, you must be willing to share your lunch time with your students. Not all schools require that you do this, but it can be quality time in which the atmosphere can be more relaxed, informal, and personal than class time usually allows.

I have never known a student, regardless of grade or age, who has not enjoyed the occasional lunch with his or her teacher. Unfortunately, too few teachers engage in this practice. (Understandably, I must add. Sometimes it is imperative that we spend a few minutes of the day around other adults. There are days when our sanity dictates this.)

First of all, determine whether behavior dictates that a specific procedure is necessary. If it is not and everything already is running smoothly, leave it alone. "Don't' fix what's not broken." If you would like a suggestion, however, here it is.

## How to Teach It

Tell your students that you will explain the lunch procedure in detail and practice it when you actually go to lunch (on this first day of school). Explain the procedure:

- Students will line up in single file and walk quietly to the cafeteria.
- Upon entering the cafeteria, the teacher will direct students to the lunch line, where they will remain in line until lunches are retrieved.
- Students then will be directed to a group of tables. (Depending on your students, you may find it necessary to group them and assign each group to a particular table.)
- Tell the students that you will sit and eat with them, rotating tables from day to day, to have the opportunity to eat and talk with each one of them at least once a week. Also tell them that even if you are not seated at their table, you will be at one nearby.
- Review the "dining rules of etiquette" with your students, as many are not familiar with them. Many of my former students had no prior experience eating in a restaurant. These are social skills that they need to be taught. Here are some examples:
  - Entering the cafeteria quietly and respectfully
  - Napkins in laps
  - Quiet tones of voice
  - Keeping their hands to themselves
  - No talking with mouths full
  - No getting in and out of seats
  - Cleanup of eating space once finished
  - Exiting the cafeteria quietly and respectfully
- Tell the students that you will remind them of these rules of etiquette in the event that they "forget."

*Note:* We will go directly to the "How to Implement It" phase of this section because our first day of implementation will be our first opportunity to practice it. Remember that it may not be pretty at first, but that's what teaching is all about. With our guidance, they'll get it. Don't give up on them. They really do want to do the right thing.

*A Word of Caution:* Some of you may be thinking that this is just for the "little kids." Depending on past behavior in the cafeteria and "what has been allowed," the older ones may need this procedure even more than the younger ones do. It's definitely harder to fix improper etiquette and behavior in the older ones because they have become accustomed to doing things a certain way. Don't neglect them. They need you!

## How to Implement It

It's time for lunch. Remind the students of the procedure. Go over the list from "How to Teach It." Allow the students to ask questions. Ask them questions. Ask them "what if" questions. Now, off to lunch.

Remember that you told the students that they were to walk quietly, in single file, on the way to the cafeteria. Don't accept anything less from them. If they don't follow this part of the procedure, go back and try it again. They're hungry. They'll do it correctly the second time.

Once in the cafeteria, continue to guide and remind them. Do not allow behaviors that are unacceptable. If you do, they will know it. Insist that they follow the procedure.

Upon returning to the classroom on that day or on the next day if this class did not return to you after lunch, praise them profusely even if there is room for improvement (and there will be—don't fool yourself). Talk first about all that was done correctly. Thank them for the experience of their company while you were eating your lunch and let them know that you look forward to this in the future.

It's all right (and vital) to talk about areas that need improvement. Have them help you brainstorm solutions for things that are still a problem. If students are given the opportunity to be part of the solution, they are much more likely to help solve the problems.

This may be a good time to talk about poor behaviors from other classes that have been observed. Without name-calling or finger-pointing, let students know that you are proud of them for being models of good behavior and that they soon will be viewed as role models for the rest of the school. Help them feel proud of their good behavior. They should be, and they deserve the praise. It's the most important part. Don't skip it!

# Procedure 24
## for Teachers and Their Students:
# Dismissing Students at Bus Time

### One, Two, Three

*Time to go now, one, two, three,*

*All you children look at me*

*Stop the talking, listen well*

*Time for the dismissal bell*

*Clean your space and pack your books*

*Tidy your desk, take coats from hooks*

*All in line now, single file*

*No talking, please; we'll wait a while*

*Okay, we're ready, one, two, three,*

*Come, now, children, follow me.*

Elizabeth Breaux

Children will leave a classroom in one of two ways: *orderly* or *chaotically*. There seems to be no middle ground. I've watched this for years. Some classes will come racing out of the building like birds released from captivity, whereas others will file out in an orderly fashion. What's the reason for the two extremes? The teacher!

*Note:* Leaving the classroom in a single-file line is not just for the little ones. It's for any child who has not learned to leave the building properly on his or her own without assistance from the teacher, regardless of how big or how old the child is.

### How to Teach It

Begin teaching this procedure about fifteen minutes before the dismissal bell on the first day of school. Tell the students that class will cease daily about five minutes before the dismissal bell. At that time they will be instructed to begin their "end of the day" tasks: pack their bags, return all class supplies, clean their spaces, and so on. They then will sit quietly.

Tell them that the class will line up in single file, beginning with the row that has completed all end of the day tasks first. (This ensures that those tasks are completed in a timely fashion.)

Once all rows have been called to line up, the teacher will allow students to move into the hallway. The teacher will lock the door, and the class will begin its journey to the bus area, the parent pickup area, the bike rider area, the day-care area, and so on, in single file.

*Note:* Schools may have their own procedures for the dismissal of students to the different areas. Whatever the procedure, what's important is that it be followed in an organized, orderly fashion.

## How to Practice It

Tell the students that there is enough time to practice the procedure once before the bell rings. Tell them that when told, they should begin performing their end of the day tasks.

Tell them that as soon as you notice that all the members of a particular row have completed all tasks satisfactorily, you will begin calling rows to line up, one row at a time.

Remind the students that they must remain orderly when in line or they will have to go back to their desks and begin the procedure again.

Ask if there are any questions. If not, begin practicing the procedure.

- Tell the students to begin their end of the day tasks.
- Call on the first row of finishers and have them line up.
- Call on the second row, third row, fourth row, and so on, until all are lined up.

If the students perform this procedure as explained during this practice session, commend them and reward them by allowing this to be the real thing. Tell them that you are proud of them. Tell them that instead of going back to their desks and starting all over, they will proceed to the bus area. Remind them to remain orderly on the way.

## How to Implement It

On the next day remind the students of the procedure again. Mentally walk through the procedure with them, reminding them of the necessary steps. Allow them to ask questions if necessary.

Implement the procedure exactly as practiced. And remember, you told them they would return to their desks and practice again if necessary. If necessary, do it! Don't let them get away with improper implementation of the procedure or they will have rewritten the procedure on these first few days of school. Be careful. If you want this to work, it's up to you to implement it properly. Now pack up and go home!

# Procedure 25
## for Teachers and Their Students:
## Implementing a Teacher Report Card

Want to know what kind of teacher you are? Ask the students. No one knows us better than they do. Go on. I dare you.

One of the best things I ever did for myself was to implement a teacher report card. I did not do this in my first years of teaching, but I wish I had, because in retrospect nothing else even came close in assisting me in my personal growth as an educator. It was truly an awesome tool, of which I would urge all teachers to take advantage.

Before you decide that this is not for you (it can be a little scary, intimidating, etc.), read on. Trust me! You're going to wonder why you waited so long.

### How to Teach It

Use of the shock factor works great for this one! On the day I first introduced this to the students (one of the first days of school), I simply projected an image of the teacher report card onto the wall with the overhead projector. I explained to my students that in nine weeks (our school system used a nine-week grading period) all the students would receive the first report card of the year. "At that time," I said to them, "you all will complete a report card on me." (Some of them looked a little stunned.) "That's correct; you will be grading me. And I want to receive straight As! I don't want you to give me an A, however, unless I truly deserve it." At this time I went through the report card with them, allowing time for discussion (see a sample on the next page).

*Teacher's name:*   Ms. Breaux     *Nine-week Period:*      1   2   3   4

_____ 1.   My teacher is well-prepared everyday.

_____ 2.   My teacher really wants me to learn.

_____ 3.   My teacher smiles a lot and says positive things.

_____ 4.   My teacher compliments my accomplishments.

_____ 5.   My teacher makes certain that I follow all school rules.

_____ 6.   My teacher does not allow me to leave class, except for emergencies.

_____ 7.   My teacher really likes me.

_____ 8.   My teacher helps me when I don't understand something.

Comments:_____

_____

Principal's signature: _____

You will want to go through everything on the report card and allow them to ask questions. They will, I assure you! There haven't been many brave souls (teachers) in their pasts who have allowed themselves to be graded by their students.

I then would reiterate to the students, "I want straight As, and I intend to do everything on the report card so that I can earn those As." (I promise that if you handle this properly, your students will love it and will be very fair in the implementation. I did this for years and never had a negative experience.)

Encourage your students to use the "Comments" section of the report card. You'll be surprised at how honest they will be and how well they know you. (A little scary sometimes.)

I remember once, years ago, when a young man wrote in the "Comments" section of the report card, "Ms. Breaux, you really need to lighten up a little." He was right. I did need to lighten up. I was much too rigid and structured and wasn't having enough fun teaching. I took his advice and started allowing myself to enjoy my students and my classes to the fullest.

Tell the students that they will see this report card again at the end of the nine-week period, when they actually fill it out for the first time. (You may want to place a copy of it somewhere in the room as a constant reminder to all of you.)

*Note:* For obvious reasons, we'll skip the "How to Practice It" part and move directly to "How to Implement It."

## How to Implement It

It's the end of the first nine-week period, and students will be receiving their own report cards. At this time you should have one teacher report card for every student you teach. As the students enter your room, again have the image projected onto the wall as a reminder, but also hand one teacher report card to each student. Emphasize that the students *are not to write their own names on these cards.* (The intention is to make them very comfortable in scoring it honestly and without concern about repercussions.)

Tell the students that you will give them a few minutes to complete the report cards and will sit at your desk to give them all the privacy they need. (Never walk around while they are completing the report cards. The idea is to make them as comfortable as possible so that they will not hesitate to be totally honest.)

Have a large manila envelope ready and ask one of the students to collect the report cards once everyone has finished. Tell the students that you will have the principal sign them. (All my administrators have been very accommodating. In fact, one of my former principals even began implementing it schoolwide, to the utter dismay of a few of the teachers. Guess which ones.)

Now take the report cards home and enjoy them. Don't forget to read the comments. They can be invaluable. And don't forget the most important part: A poor grade means that you have work to do. Listen to the students. They know you so well!

# Conclusion

### I Teach

*I light a spark in a darkened soul*
*I warm the heart of one grown cold*
*I look beyond and see within*
*Behind the face, beneath the skin*
*I quench a thirst, I soothe a pain*
*I provide the food that will sustain*
*I touch, I love, I laugh, I cry*
*Whatever is needed I supply*
*Yet more than I give, I gain from each.*
*I am most richly blessed....I teach.*

*Annette Breaux*

From: *"New Teacher Induction"*

Teachers...

You truly hold the keys to the futures of your students. It is not books, nor is it programs, but the effectiveness of you, their teacher. You are their bottom line. You may be the most powerful person in many of their lives. Do not ever take that role lightly. You are amongst those of us who have chosen a most noble profession that carries with it a wealth of responsibility. Handle it, and them, with the utmost of care...